TREES OF THE WORLD

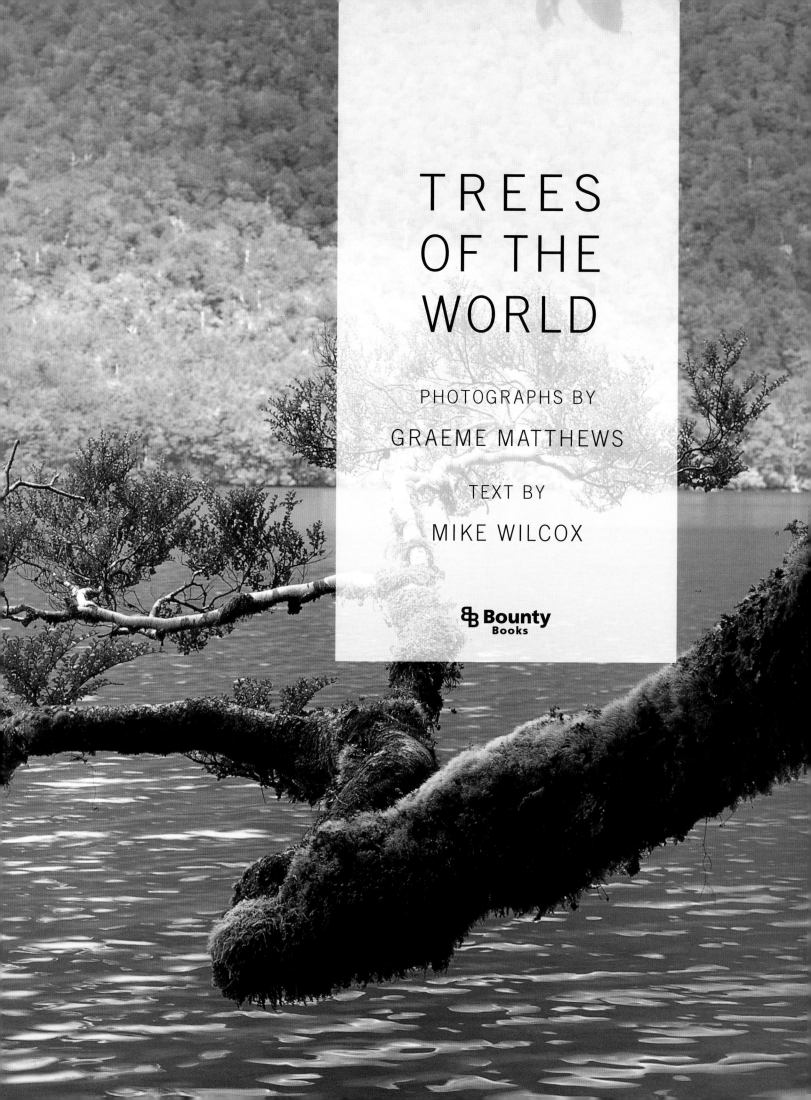

TREES OF THE WORLD

PHOTOGRAPHS BY

GRAEME MATTHEWS

TEXT BY

MIKE WILCOX

B Bounty
Books

HALF TITLE PAGE: **Black Forest, Germany**

TITLE PAGE: **Lake Christabel, South Island, New Zealand**

THIS PAGE: **Oirase Valley, Honshu, Japan**

CONTENTS PAGE: **Kokerboom Forest, Namibia**

BACK PAGE: **Farmland, Wales**

Copyright © photography Graeme Matthews, 2006
Copyright © David Bateman Ltd, 2006

First published 2006 by David Bateman Ltd, 30 Tarndale Grove, Albany, Auckland, New Zealand

This edition published 2006 by Bounty Books, a division of Octopus Publishing Group Ltd, 2-4 Heron Quays, London E14 4JP

ISBN-13: 978 0 753713 47 1
ISBN-10: 0753713 47 0

Designed by Jag Graphics, Auckland, New Zealand

Printed in China

CONTENTS

Introduction   8

The trees of Europe   16

The trees of Asia   52

The trees of Africa   74

The trees of North America   98

The trees of South America   124

The trees of Oceania   140

Appendix : Some national and state trees   156

Index   158

INTRODUCTION by Mike Wilcox

Trees have always been important to people, and occur everywhere on land where the climate is warm and moist enough to support their survival and growth. They have three main parts – a crown of foliage, a woody trunk, and a root system. The crown has branches bearing green leaves which absorb carbon dioxide from the air and convert it by photosynthesis into cellulose and lignin, the main components of wood. The woody trunk has an intricate vascular system to conduct water up from the roots to the top of the tree and food downwards from the photosynthetic crown. The roots anchor the tree to the soil and absorb water and mineral nutrients from the soil, the most important being nitrogen and phosphorus. Reproductive structures are borne in the crown.

Trees are usually long lived and grow in height and diameter year by year. While the growing period in the wet tropics may be continuous, in the dry tropics growth occurs mainly in the wet season of just a few months, and is likewise restricted by cold on high mountains and in the far northern latitudes subject to permafrost. In many areas of the world where there is a strong seasonality in temperature and rainfall, many species of trees form distinct annual growth rings. As more and more rings grow over the lifetime of these trees, they form a record of year-by-year changes in climate, often stretching across hundreds and sometimes thousands of years.

EVOLUTION

Spore-bearing trees

Trees first appeared on earth in the middle Devonian period, 380 million years ago. These earliest trees were lycopods (such as *Lepidodendron*) that reproduced by spores, had branches, a root system, bark, a vascular system, and grew to an impressive 35 metres (115 feet) in height and 1 metre (3 feet) in diameter. They dominated the forests of the Carboniferous period (290–315 million years ago), forming the rich coal deposits which give that geological period its name. The arborescent lycopod experiment was obviously not completely successful because lycopods persist throughout the world to the present day just as small plants. Another kind of ancient spore-bearing tree from this early time was the giant 20-metre (66 feet) tall horsetail tree (*Calamites*), again destined to persist in present times as the small horsetails (*Equisetum*). It co-existed with ferns; the ancient tree fern *Psaronius* attained a height of 10 metres (32 feet). Today there are 500 species of modern tree ferns in the world, with species of *Cyathea* having trunks 20 metres (66 feet) tall.

The next trees to develop were still spore-bearing but had some gymnosperm-like features as well. These so-called progymnosperms, of which *Archaeopteris* is a representative, had flattened foliage, a woody stem with growth rings rather like those of conifers, and a well-formed root system. It was perhaps the first truly woody tree. There are no trees of this type still alive today.

The earliest seed-producing trees

Two groups of seed plants date back 360 million years to the early Carboniferous period. These were the seed ferns and the Cordaitales – the first of the gymnosperms, with woody trunks, pollen borne in sporangia, and, very significantly, the female egg enclosed in an ovule, which developed into a seed.

The Permian period, 290 to 248 million years ago, saw the proliferation of the seed ferns and Cordaitales, and the emergence of other gymnosperms, notably cycads, *Ginkgo* and its relatives, the cycad-like Bennetitales, and the glossopterids, this latter group being seed ferns that dominated the Permian forests of the great southern continent, Gondwana. Only the cycads and *Ginkgo* still exist today, with *Ginkgo biloba* of China being the oldest of all living trees. Living cycads can grow quite tall, notably the 20-metre (66-foot) tall *Lepidozamia hopei* of tropical Queensland, Australia, and can also claim to be trees.

Conifers

There are some 630 species of conifer in the world today – by far the dominant group of living gymnosperms. Conifers arose in the Upper Carboniferous period, c. 310 million years ago, and evolved and spread abundantly during the Mesozoic (beginning 248 million years ago), with all families well differentiated by the Jurassic period (206–144 million years ago). Today coniferous trees dominate large expanses of forests in the colder regions of the Northern Hemisphere, and are well represented on all continents, including in the tropics. They are indeed trees of the world, and some of them like the coast redwood (*Sequoia sempervirens*), the giant redwood (*Sequoiadendron giganteum*), the Douglas fir (*Pseudotsuga menziesii*), the Sitka spruce (*Picea sitchensis*), the New Zealand kauri (*Agathis australis*), and the Mexican bald cypress (*Taxodium mucronatum*) grow to a great age and size. The Tulé cypress ('El Árbol de Tule') in Oaxaca, Mexico, is a huge Mexican bald cypress thought to be more than 2000 years old. Its massive trunk has a gross girth of 54 metres (178 feet) and a diameter of about 14.3 metres (47 feet). Its height is just over 40 metres (132 feet), and it has an estimated wood volume of 817 cubic metres (28,852 cubic feet).

ABOVE: **Ginkgo (*Ginkgo biloba*), Hirosaki, Japan**

RIGHT: **Kauri (*Agathis australis*), Waipoua Forest, New Zealand**

BELOW: **Tree ferns, New Zealand**

BELOW LEFT: **Zuurberg cycad, Zuurberg National Park, South Africa**

Angiosperms

The angiosperms or flowering plants are the most abundant and diverse group of plants in the world. From their first known ancestral origins in the Cretaceous period (65–44 million years ago), they have evolved into an enormous array of families, genera and species, and also numerous life forms, ranging from tiny herbs, desert succulents and aquatic plants, to parasites, epiphytes, climbers, shrubs, and trees. Loosely defined as woody plants growing 8 metres (26 feet) or more tall, trees number about 80,000 species of the total 250,000 or so angiosperm species in the world. Two broad categories of angiosperm trees are recognised – the monocotyledons (monocots) and the dicotyledons (dicots). The monocot trees have strap-like or frond-like foliage with parallel veins, borne atop a slender, cylindrical, fibrous stem, typical examples being the palms, the dracaenas, yuccas, and cabbage trees (*Cordyline*). The dicot or broadleaved trees have true wood in their trunks, with foliage comprising leaves of various shapes and sizes.

Mountain forest, Urewera National Park, New Zealand

WHERE TREES GROW

Trees need moisture to survive and grow, and they get this by growing either in moist climates or damp sites, or in arid regions by sending down roots deep enough to reach the underground water table. Most trees grow in forests as pure stands of single species or mixed stands of numerous species. In some forests (such as rainforest) it is possible to find tree ferns, cycads, conifers, palms, and woody dicot trees all growing together in a complex ecosystem, with a dense overhead canopy 40–50 metres (130–165 feet) above the ground. Other forests are seemingly simpler in structure, notably the *Eucalyptus* forests of Australia with few other kinds of trees present, the northern boreal coniferous forests comprising just a few species of *Pinus*, *Larix*, *Picea* or *Abies*, interspersed with broadleaved trees such as birch (*Betula*) and poplar (*Populus*), the *Nothofagus* mountain forests of New Zealand and Chile, and the mangrove forests of tropical rivers and estuaries.

As well as closed-canopy forests, trees naturally occur in much more open types of vegetation. In dry regions, trees may be confined to river banks, as with *Eucalyptus camaldulensis* – that famous eucalypt of inland Australia – and *Populus euphratica* and *Platanus orientalis* of central Asia. Much of central Africa is covered in savannah woodland comprising grassy vegetation with scattered trees, like the flat-topped, thorny *Acacia*. The Miombo region of southern and eastern Africa has a long dry season of up to nine months over the cooler part of the year. Miombo woodlands occupy vast areas of flat land on nutrient-poor soils and are subject to fires. The trees are scattered and mostly deciduous, generally from 8 to 15 metres (26–49 feet) tall, with *Brachystegia* and *Julbernandia* of the legume sub-family Caesalpinioideae being highly characteristic.

ABOVE: **Poplars, Alphen, Netherlands**

LEFT: **Acacia trees, Central Africa**

IMPORTANCE OF TREES

People make many uses of trees. Forests of trees provide products such as timber, firewood, bark fibres, medicines and chemical products; they provide food and shelter for animals; they provide a protective cover to the land, retaining soil and regulating water supply; and they provide scenery and a place for recreation and spiritual contemplation.

Of all the 80,000 kinds of tree, just a very few have been brought into cultivation and domesticated for man's use. Some, like the coconut palm (*Cocos nucifera*), are grown throughout the tropics. Such trees yield numerous products from the stem, foliage and fruit. As for forestry plantations, throughout the world the most widely grown are a few species of *Eucalyptus*, *Pinus*, *Populus*, and *Acacia*. Rubber (*Hevea brasiliensis*) is a tree of great economic importance for the latex it yields, and there are innumerable trees grown in both temperate regions (e.g. apple, pear, and peach, orange, walnut) and the tropics (e.g. mango, rambutan and cashew nut) for fruits and nuts. In addition to economic trees, a great many trees have been cultivated for ornamental and amenity purposes in our villages, towns, cities, and on farms, giving such benefits as shade, shelter, visual screening, barriers to sound, and general greenery. Every city in the world has an arboretum, botanical garden, or tree collection of some sort, where trees have been brought together. Some great ornamental flowering trees of the tropics are rain tree (*Samanea saman*), poinciana (*Delonix regia*), and jacaranda (*Jacaranda mimosifolia*).

Walnut tree (*Juglans regia*)

ABOVE: **Forestry plantation, New Zealand**

LEFT: **Logged pine and logging ship**

Drakensberg Mountains,
South Africa

IMMIGRANT TREES

The trees illustrated in this book are mostly shown in their natural, wild setting, but trees are great travellers and have been transported and transplanted by man far beyond their native homes. Why do people plant trees? The practical reasons are obvious – for edible fruit, for shelter and shade against wind and sun, for wood, to stabilise soil along river banks and on steep slopes, and to restore or regenerate destroyed forests. Trees are also much planted in gardens, city streets and in parks, arboreta, school grounds, campuses and cemeteries to display their beauty, to give vertical structure to the landscape, and to commemorate the dead. City managers everywhere have to attend to their trees, and they commonly have to deal with conflicts. Trees planted in the wrong place can make a nuisance of themselves by interfering with overhead power and telephone wires, by the roots getting into drains and damaging driveways, by the leaves littering the ground and clogging up drainpipes, by blocking views, and by being a danger to traffic.

Unfortunately some immigrant trees have gone well beyond the domesticated confines of gardens and parks and become naturalised in their new homes, often as serious economic and environmental weeds. Florida in the USA has swamps infested with the Australian broadleaf paperbark (*Melaleuca quinquenervia*) and also she-oak (*Casuarina equisetifolia*, *C. glauca*, *C. cunninghamiana*), while tree of heaven (*Ailanthus altissima*) from China is thoroughly naturalised in both western and eastern USA. Southern Europe's most notorious invader is perhaps silver wattle (*Acacia dealbata*) from Australia, while South Africa has a long list of Australian invaders, especially *Acacia*. As the examples show, Australia has been the source of many invasive weeds, but also has some immigrant problem trees of its own such as the Chinese camphor (*Cinnamomum camphora*) which has colonised disturbed rainforest in New South Wales and Queensland.

In New Caledonia, *Leucaena leucocephala* from Central America has colonised hillsides on the western coast. New Zealand has many examples, such as tree privet (*Ligustrum lucidum*) from China, Cape Leeuwin or lillypilly (*Acmena smithii*) from Australia, maritime pine (*Pinus pinaster*), crack willow (*Salix fragilis*) and grey willow (*Salix cinerea*) from Europe, and lodgepole pine (*Pinus contorta*) from North America. The Pacific Islands also have several serious woody weed invaders, including candle nut (*Aleurites moluccana*) and guava (*Psidium guajava*).

ABOVE: **Plane trees, Hangzchou, China**

RIGHT: **African woodland, here devastated by elephants**

BOTTOM LEFT: **Sheffield Park, England**

TREE HEALTH AND PROTECTION

Trees are important components of savannah and forest ecosystems, providing shelter and habitats for animals, including browsers on the foliage. However, sometimes the natural checks and balances are disrupted, and browsers explode in numbers and become pests, devouring and killing the very food plants they depend on. Pathogenic fungi and bacteria can also severely debilitate trees, as is sometimes experienced in large man-made forestry plantations and horticultural fruit orchards, and in forest trees weakened by physiological stress. There have been historical tree plagues that have just about wiped out some species, namely the demise of American chestnut (*Castanea dentata*). This once valuable hardwood timber tree in eastern North America, with forests of huge trees, was all but destroyed by chestnut blight (*Endothia parasitica*). The blight arrived in New York from Asia in 1904, and spread southwards. By 1930, the magnificent chestnut forests of the Appalachians had been wiped out. Its place in the forest appears to have been taken by *Quercus rubra*. Another famous tree plague is Dutch elm disease which all but obliterated American elm (*Ulmus americana*) in America and wych elm (*Ulmus glabra*), Dutch elm (*Ulmus* x *hollandica*) and common elm (*Ulmus procera*) in Europe.

Climatic events can also do great damage to trees. The eastern states of North America sometimes experience ice storms so severe that the tops and branches of large trees are broken to pieces or the whole tree brought down under the sheer weight of accumulated ice. Tropical cyclones are equally destructive. The modern industrial world is subject to large-scale atmospheric pollution in the form of 'acid rain', in which gases such as sulphur dioxide and nitrous oxide reach levels sufficient to injure foliage and weaken trees, making them more susceptible to pests and diseases. Such forest health decline is the cause of great concern and anxiety as people sense their environment is unhealthy when trees are dying around them. Of even greater concern is the rapid, unprecedented rise in the level of carbon dioxide in the atmosphere over the last 50 years, from 250 ppm to 380 ppm, leading to global warming with high likelihood of drastic effects on trees, and the environment generally. Governments are attempting to reduce gaseous emissions by limiting energy consumption and at the same time encouraging the planting of 'carbon' forests to help absorb the excess carbon dioxide.

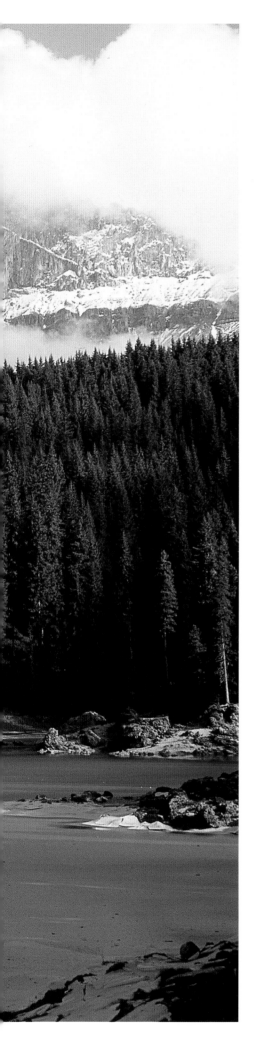

THE TREES
OF EUROPE

O f all the main continental land masses, Europe, with its long history of human occupation, has by far the fewest kinds of tree, and the most modified forests. The ice ages eliminated much of what was once a rich flora, but there are nonetheless still some extensive forests, particularly in the high mountains. The Black Forest (Schwarzwald) in Germany of 5000 square kilometres (1930 square miles) is one of Europe's largest tracts of trees, containing oak and beech woods together with spruce and fir. One of the best remaining lowland forests in Europe is the Bialowieza National Park in Poland, with primeval mixed forest of pine, beech, oak, alder and spruce, together with lime, hornbeam, elm, ash, and maple. The forest dates back to 8000 BC and is the only remaining example of the original forests which once covered much of Europe. One third of the Bialowieza is located in Poland, with the remainder in Belarus. In Britain there are still some 700 square kilometres (270 square miles) of wild upland oak woods dominated by sessile oak (*Quercus petraea*).

Turning first to the conifers, Scots pine (*Pinus sylvestris*) is a highly characteristic tree of European forests, and stretches from Scotland through Scandinavia, central and eastern Europe, Turkey, and across Russia all the way to northeast China. With its reddish, flaking bark and usually bluish, short needles, it is a tree of great beauty as well as yielding a commercial timber of considerable importance.

Another European conifer is the black pine (*Pinus nigra*), which is found in four distinctive subspecies from the Pyrenees to eastern Turkey, with the Corsican pine (*P. nigra* subsp. *laricio*) having a particularly good reputation in timber plantations in England. Four other species of pines have a more Mediterranean occurrence – Aleppo pine (*Pinus halepensis*), Turkish pine (*P. brutia*), maritime pine (*P. pinaster*), and stone pine (*P. pinea*). Respighi's musical symphonic poem, the *Pines of Rome*, was inspired by stone pines, which are much used for their edible seeds. In the European Alps can be found the Swiss stone pine or Arolla pine (*Pinus cembra*) and the Swiss mountain pine (*P. mugo*) – commonly just a prostrate shrub. Bosnian pine (*Pinus heldreichii*) and Macedonian pine (*P. peuce*) are found in the Balkans, and *P. canariensis* is a noble species confined to the Canary Islands.

The cold mountains of Europe are home to several other conifers, the three best known being European larch (*Larix europaea*), Norway spruce (*Picea abies*), and European white fir (*Abies alba*). Larch is a feature of the European alps of France, Switzerland, Italy, Germany and Austria, with major tracts also in the Carpathian Mountains of southern Poland and Slovenia. Spruce has an immense distribution, extending from eastern France through central and eastern Europe, the Nordic countries, and Russia. Fir occurs in the Pyrenees and eastwards to central Europe and down into Italy and the Balkans.

Norway spruce (*Picea abies*), Dolomites, northeastern Italy

Norway spruce is one of the best known of the conifers that grow in the cold mountain regions of Europe.

Further representatives of the pine family (Pinaceae) in Europe and adjoining Turkey and the Caucasus are oriental spruce (*Picea orientalis*), Serbian spruce (*P. omorika*), Caucasian fir (*Abies nordmanniana*), Spanish fir (*A. pinsapo*), Taurus fir (*A. cilicica*), Grecian fir (*A. cephalonica*) and cedar of Lebanon (*Cedrus libani*). The cypress family (Cupressaceae) has the well-known Mediterranean cypress (*Cupressus sempervirens*), most commonly seen in its slender form so characteristic of churchyards and towns of southern Europe, and also several kinds of juniper, ranging from prostrate alpine shrubs such as *Juniperus communis* and *oxycedrus*, to trees like the Syrian juniper (*J. drupacea*), which has edible fruits, also *J. foetidissima* and the massive-trunked Greek juniper (*J. excelsa*).

The native broadleaved trees of Europe are primarily deciduous, the only evergreens being several confined mainly to the interesting scrubby vegetation of the Mediterranean in the areas known as maquis. Here can be found the bay laurel (*Laurus nobilis*), holm oak (*Quercus ilex*), kermes oak (*Q. coccifera*), holly (*Ilex aquifolium*), evergreen buckthorn (*Rhamnus alaternus*), carob (*Ceratonia siliqua*) and the strawberry tree (*Arbutus unedo*). Southern Europe's most revered tree is undoubtedly the olive (*Olea europaea*), much cultivated for its oil-yielding fruit, as is cork oak (*Quercus suber*) for its bark. Cherry laurel (*Prunus laurocerasus*) is another evergreen, found in the higher rainfall forests such as those bordering the Black Sea in Turkey.

Europe's deciduous trees are among the best known and appreciated of all the world's trees. European beech (*Fagus sylvatica*) and its eastern extension, *F. orientalis*, form pure beautiful beech woods. Beech is the chosen National Tree of Great Britain, and is a fine furniture wood. Chestnut (*Castanea sativa*), pedunculate oak (*Quercus robur*) and sessile oak (*Q. petraea*) are familiar, common European trees of the family. In the coldest northern regions of Europe, birch (*Betula pubescens* and *B. pendula*) are widespread. Birch is the National Tree of Russia, and a Russian proverb praises four possible ways of using its products: torches of birch wood, grease from birch tar, tea of birch leaves, and birch switches to clean the body. Birch is commonly accompanied by aspen (*Populus tremula*); their relative, alder (*Alnus glutinosa*) shows a distinct preference for river banks and wetland margins. The ashes (*Fraxinus excelsior* and *F. angustifolia)* and willows such as crack willow (*Salix fragilis*) likewise grow on damp, fertile sites. Other familiar European deciduous trees are rowan (*Sorbus aucuparia*), whitebeam (*S. aria*), linden or common lime (*Tilia* x *europaea*), field maple (*Acer campestre*), sycamore maple (*A. pseudoplatanus*), Norway maple (*A. platanoides*), various elms (*Ulmus x hollandica, U. glabra, U. carpinifolia, U. laevis*), hornbeam (*Carpinus betulus*) and black poplar (*Populus nigra*).

Snowdonia National Park, Wales

The park covers 2154 square kilometres (832 square miles). It has fine examples of wild upland Atlantic oak woods dominated by sessile oak (*Quercus petraea*), together with ash (*Fraxinus excelsior*), rowan (*Sorbus aucuparia*), downy birch (*Betula pubescens*), and hazel (*Corylus avellana*).

Ancient relict Scots pine (*Pinus sylvestris*), Scotland

Scots pine is found growing across an area that extends from Scotland through Scandinavia to Central and Eastern Europe, Turkey and across Russia as far as northeastern China.

Eng Valley, Karwendel Mountains, Austria

The woods are made for the hunters of dreams.
— Sam Walter Foss

Where the fields end, the dark forests begin. Throughout old European and British folklore, to enter the forest was to enter a realm of tree spirits, undefined fears and the haunting unknown. Beyond the risks of encounters with wolves and other wild animals that once lived in the great forests, were the less defined but equally terrifying possibilities of meeting fairy folk. A host of rituals was developed to placate tree spirits and other legendary denizens of the forest who might otherwise lead a traveller or woodcutter to their death. All over Europe, protection against the forest spirits was the same—wear one's clothes inside out and put one's shoes on the wrong feet.

Fontainebleau Forest, France

Covering 250 square kilometres (96 square miles), Fontainebleau Forest is a vestige of the old forests of France. It is situated close to Paris and was the favoured hunting ground of French rulers from Louis IX to Napoleon III. Since the 1800s, the forest has been sectioned by an orderly pattern of paths which lead the visitor through grand boulevards, avenues and crossroads arched by oak, beech and pine — the most common canopy trees at Fontainebleau. There is a tradition linking the leaf-filtered light and peaceful grace of Fontainebleau with great French painters — Rousseau, Millet, Monet and Renoir, among others — who visited the forest for artistic inspiration.

Mediterranean cypress, Umbria, Italy

The dark green spire of the Mediterranean cypress (*Cupressus sempervirens*), while native to all of southeastern Europe and western Asia, is symbolic of central Italy. With its moisture-conserving, closed-umbrella shape and small, scale-like leaves, it is a tree perfectly adapted to survive the hot, dry summers and mild, moist winters of this region. The timber of the cypress was used by the Romans, who valued its strength for building houses, temples and sea-going galleys. Because of the fragrant natural oils in its wood, the Mediterranean cypress is often used to make clothes chests.

Cypresses, Tuscany, Italy

Neuschwanstein Castle, Bavaria, Germany

In a dream I conceived it; my will called it into being.
Strong and fair it stands, a fortress proud and peerless.
— Wotan on building Valhalla in Wagner's opera *Das Rheingold*

A castle to match the romance and mysticism evoked by the wild forests of Bavaria, Neuschwanstein was designed by the architect Reidel for Ludwig II of Bavaria. Within its stone turrets the king could escape to a life of medieval make-believe amid the forested mountains. Ludwig II maintained a close friendship with Wagner, providing both money and inspiration for the composer. Wagner's operas in turn gave a physical reality to Ludwig's own internal dream world. The king's architectural fantasies came close to bankrupting the Bavarian government until finally a medical commission plotted to prove Ludwig II insane and he was forced to give up his throne. His unfinished castle remains, a symbol of the magical dreams that have been drawn from the forested mountains of southern Germany.

Hills of Umbria, Italy

English oak, Hampshire, England

England has taken to its heart the oak tree, honouring through history its sheltering beauty and strong timber. The Druids of Celtic Britain believed the oak to be sacred and their secret rites used mistletoe from its boughs. Oak built the British throne as well as the ships of the fleets that were sent across the oceans in war and exploration. Seven hundred large oaks might be required for the construction of one ship. By Elizabeth I's reign, the felling of oak had become so extensive that laws had to be passed to protect the tree.

Today, oaks are a major component of woodland all over the lowland counties and on the lower slopes of many hills in the north and west. The oak remains central to the vision of the classical English landscape.

*It was forests of tall trees like this one with its intertwining branches that gave the architects of the
Middle Ages their inspiration for their cathedral vaults. The leaves that fall in the autumn, the sap
that rises in the spring — is that not, after all, the symbol of the life to come?*
— Rosa Bonheur

ABOVE: **St Koloman's Church, Romantic Road, Germany**

Eng Valley, Karwendel Mountains, Austria

Beneath the snow, frozen water is locked in the ground and no moisture can be drawn by the trees to replace that lost through transpiration. Above ground, winds howl with bitter strength across the land. Trees have diverged in the way they deal with the difficult conditions of winter. The evergreen softwoods have their narrow leaves coated with wax and impregnated with resins to minimise water loss during times when little is available. They are able to wait out winter while conserving their deep green foliage. Their tapering slender habits are designed to survive storms and gales.

However if the hardwood tree at the centre of this picture had kept its thin-skinned, broad-bladed leaves throughout the winter, it would have died of drought as transpiration drew away the last of its irreplaceable moisture. The open canopy of branches could not have survived winter storms bearing a great burden of leaves. For this reason hardwoods shed their leaves in autumn and let the winds rip through their empty limbs. These two approaches to winter are both successful in the middle latitudes of Europe.

BELOW: **Pine, Bavaria, Germany**

You know the mountain range and its cloudy path?
The mule seeks its way there in the mist;
the ancient brood of dragons dwells in caves;
the cliff falls sheer and the stream over it.
— Johann Wolfgang von Goethe

RIGHT: **Karwendel Mountains, Austria**

This Biogenetic Reserve of 540 square kilometres (208 square miles) features Norway spruce, larch, Arolla pine and mountain pine, with beech at lower elevations.

Birches and pines, Glen Affric, Scotland

Glen Affric contains one of the last stands of old Caledonian wildwood. Typical of the Scottish Highlands' forest, Scots pine and birch are the most common trees at Glen Affric. In early pre-history, such forest covered most of the eastern and middle Highlands of Scotland, but by the time of the earliest documents they were already rare. Tillage and the creation of pasture ate away at the forests. Today, much of this land is covered in blanket peat, probably largely as a result of the destruction of the wildwoods. Despite the remnant size of the Caledonian woodlands, they are not wholly safe from continued destruction. Some are still threatened by overgrazing or with the planting of non-native conifers.

Pines, Sheffield Park, England

The beauty of the setting sun is made more ruby by the pollution of these urban skies. Sulphur dioxide from industrial wastes creates acid rain, which will eventually destroy the forests of Europe unless controlled. The air pollution brought to the earth by rain has already caused a reduction in the variety of lichens that grow on city trees.

Black Forest, Germany

Twenty-nine percent of German land is forested. The species composition of much of this forest is not natural, however. It is managed for the production of the most valuable timber species, particularly spruce. On many sites, spruce is a pioneering species that will not regenerate under its own canopy. Instead, if left to nature, the forest's composition will gradually change as shade-tolerant beech seedlings grow under a spruce canopy, eventually overtopping and dominating the spruce. In managed forest, foresters clear regenerating beech and promote the replacement of spruce. Only in specially created reserves does the original forest of southern Germany now survive.

European larches, Switzerland

The larch belongs to a small conifer genus found throughout the northern world. Larches are among the very few softwoods that lose their leaves over winter. Designed to withstand blizzards and avalanches, larches are found on the higher slopes of the Alps. Unlike other conifers, their needle-like leaves, noted for their softness, need only survive a single summer.

Beech and silver firs, Black Forest, Germany

'Where does a wise man hide a leaf?'
And the other answered: 'In the forest'.
—G.K. Chesterton

During the long, warm days of summer, deciduous trees must maximise their use of the sun's energy for their leaves are soon dropped with the change of the season. Colours turn in the leaves as the tree lays down corky layers at the leaf stalk, gradually cutting off the flow of sap until the leaf dies and falls. Yellow, red and purple pigments are revealed as the residual foods in the leaf are returned to the tree, and then a deciduous forest is aflame with dying autumn colour.

ABOVE: **Spruce and alder forest, Lake Mjøsa, Norway**

The forests of Scandinavia are part of the taiga — a circumpolar high-latitude forest which stretches almost without interruption across the continents of Eurasia and North America. It is dominated by conifers: species of spruce, pine, fir and larch. The species mix changes across countries and with small-scale variations in growing conditions, although they all excel in surviving the long, bitterly cold winters of the far north.

RIGHT: **Rowan berries, Vestfold, Norway**

Rowan (or mountain ash), from the rose family, is distributed widely through Europe and also in parts of Asia and North Africa. Something about its strongly ascending branches, its lacy foliage or the masses of its striking red berries has connected it with witchcraft from ancient times. Its very name, rowan, is believed to be derived from the Norse word *runa*, meaning 'charm'. Rowan trees were often planted outside houses and in churchyards to ward off witches.

ABOVE: **Birch forest, Varmland, Sweden**

Birch is a short-lived pioneer tree, breaking ground for the forest returning after disturbance. In this role, it was the first common tree to appear after the glaciers retreated and the continental ice sheets began to melt at the close of the ice ages in Europe. For a time, between 10,000 and 5000 years ago, birch trees so dominated the landscape that those millennia are often referred to as the Birch Period. Birch is a natural symbol of restoration and this role was reflected in the reverence in which the Celtic and Germanic tribes held the tree. To them, the birch was holy, with powers of renewal and purification.

In the dominant birch forests of the post ice age, early Europeans used many parts of the tree. Its bark was peeled off and sewn like fine leather for clothing, or moulded for canoes; the cambium tissue was ground to make bread and the sap fermented to make mead; its pitch glued spears and its bark made roofing tiles. And, under its lightly cast shade, a forest may return.

RIGHT: **Ash, North Yorkshire Dales, England**

The ash tree (*Fraxinus excelsior*) occurs throughout Great Britain. Its timber is renowned for its strength and resilience, and much used for tool handles.

Beech, Hinterriss, Austria

Old, character-filled trees like this beech have inspired myths of 'life-source' trees, such as Yggdrasill, the Cosmic Tree of Norse/Germanic origin. Yggdrasill was a great ash. One of its three roots reached to the Spring of Fate, the second to the Spring of Wisdom, the third to the source of all rivers and the Land of the Dead. From its boughs, which encompassed earth and heaven, fell the dew.

In a second story of Scandinavian origin, men are descended from an ash tree and women from an elm. Odin and his brothers gave the two trees souls and life, the wit and will to move, then faces, speech, sight and hearing. The human race is descended from these two trees.

Loch Awe, Scotland

Although the photograph reflects the sparse growth characteristic of the Scottish Highlands, nearby Inverliever and Eredine Forests between them extend to about 20 square kilometres (7.7 square miles).

The Dolomite Mountains rise in the eastern section of the northern Italian Alps. Formed from dolomite limestone, they have been deeply carved by erosion to form steep rock faces, gorges and pinnacles. On many of the easier scree slopes, patches of forest are found.

RIGHT: **Olive tree, Tuscany, Italy**

The olive, cultivated since prehistoric times, is a native of Asia Minor and Syria. Given its languid growth and the great age it reaches (between 1000 and 1500 years), it is not surprising that the olive is a symbol of peace.

Hedgerows, Wales

The composition of a hedgerow can reveal the complex history of its use and development. Generally, the older a hedgerow, the more species-rich it is. As well, in different periods of history people have favoured different hedgerow plants. An ancient hedgerow will often have giant coppiced trees; hedges of the Tudor age are identified by their maple and dogwood; pre-Tudor hedges feature hazel and spindle; and in a post-1800 hedge hawthorn is common. Individual trees are often distinguished and remembered — marked by a heavy bearing of lichens, or by crooked limbs, or as an unusually bright bearer of berries, or by burls and epiphytes. The drive for efficiency in farming has seen the clearance of many ancient hedges, although they are increasingly being defended for their species richness and their illustrative living histories.

Beech, Scotland

With its stately form, strong silver branches and deeply cast shade, the beech tree is sometimes called the 'Queen of the Forest'. It is not native to Scotland (or anywhere north of the Midlands), but has been widely planted there. Beech prefers more difficult conditions than oak, and in the south is dominant in the woods of the chalky uplands. A single beech tree can support 200 different kinds of invertebrates.

Villandry Chateau, Loire Valley, France, Yew Topiary

Topiary, the art of ornamental tree pruning, is said to have been invented by a friend of the Roman emperor Augustus and is known to have been practised in the first century AD. The fashion reached its height in the late seventeenth and early eighteenth centuries, but faded when interest turned to the natural garden. Thickly-leaved evergreen trees like cypress, yew and box respond best to being shaped by pruning.

ABOVE: **Norway maple, Vestfold, Norway**

The Norway maple (*Acer platanoides*) is one of three species of maple found naturally in the forests of Europe. It is the hardiest of the European maples, well suited to life in the far northern forests of its Scandinavian home.

RIGHT: **Spruces, larches and beech trees, Switzerland**

In Switzerland, the character of these wooded landscapes is preserved by ordinances which prevent private landowners felling too many trees at any one time. The beautiful landscape is completed with stone walls and grapevines.

THE TREES OF ASIA

2

Asia is exceedingly rich in trees, covering as it does a wide range of habitats from the tropics to the Arctic north. China, Japan, Korea and the Russian Far East together form a great tree region, rich in both conifers and broadleaves. The traveller in southeastern China will quickly become familiar with Masson pine (*Pinus massoniana*) and Chinese fir (*Cunninghamia lanceolata*), both much cultivated for timber. A trip up the Yellow Mountains in Anhui Province will bring the visitor in touch with the famous Yellow Mountain pine (*Pinus taiwanensis*) sitting picture-postcard style atop vertical cliffs. The related Chinese red pine (*Pinus tabuliformis*) occurs in drier, colder regions in northern China, and its southern counterparts in Yunnan are *Pinus yunnanensis* and *P. densata*. Numerous species of the deciduous larches (*Larix*) can be found, together with spruces (*Picea*) and *Abies*. Two Chinese conifers of special interest are ginkgo (*Ginkgo biloba*) — China's State Tree — and dawn redwood (*Metasequoia glyptostroboides*).

Compared with China's twenty percent tree cover, Japan still has an impressive sixty percent of its land in forests, consisting of a high diversity of conifers – firs (*Abies*), spruces (*Picea*), larch (*Larix*), pines (*Pinus*), and some very noble, valuable timber species of the cypress family, notably sugi (*Cryptomeria japonica*) and hinoki (*Chamaecyparis obtusa*). Japan also has numerous deciduous trees, with the maples and oaks being particularly common.

Teak (*Tectona grandis*) is a deciduous tree found in tropical monsoonal Asia where there is an alternating distinct dry season and rainy reason. It is perhaps the most admired of all tropical timbers and the standard against which all other timbers are judged, combining as it does the qualities of stability, durability and attractive grain. The best natural teak stands are to be found in Myanmar and Thailand, but many countries including India, Sri Lanka and Indonesia (mainly in Java) grow teak in plantations.

The traveller in central and southern India and Sri Lanka will see many other trees of great social and economic significance to the people. These include neem (*Azadirachta indica*), with natural insecticidal properties; tamarind (*Tamarindus indica*), from which the pulp in the pods is used every day in Indian curries; the jakfruit (*Artocarpus heterophyllus*), grown in home gardens for shade, shelter, fruit, and timber; and the ubiquitous mango (*Mangifera indica*) — a magnificent shade and ornamental tree as well as bearing delicious fruit.

Sri Lanka in 1986 chose one of its rainforest trees, na or ironwood (*Mesua ferrea*) as its National Tree. It has beautiful flowers, an immensely heavy, strong wood, and it is believed that the first visit of Buddha was to grove of a na trees at Miyanganaya and also the next Buddha (mithriya) will attain enlightenment under a na tree. The flower of na is also used in herbal medicine and preparation of perfumes, cosmetics and soaps.

Liquidambar, Oirase, Northern Honshu, Japan

India's National Tree is the banyan (*Ficus benghalensis*) – a tree often of huge proportions with aerial roots forming a great curtain surrounding the main stem. The figs (*Ficus*) are prominent trees throughout Asia, and the bo tree (*Ficus religiosa*) has special significance for Buddhists.

The dipterocarps constitute a family of strictly tropical trees numbering 16 genera and 515 species stretching from India to New Guinea. There are 267 species alone in Borneo, and 155 in peninsular Malaysia. They constitute the single most important group of Asian timber trees, furnishing around eighty percent of the Southeast Asia log business. Important genera are *Shorea*, *Dryobalanops* and *Dipterocarpus*, with *Shorea* providing most of the region's utility timber, generally known as meranti. While actually grasses, the bamboos attain such a size and yield such a wide range of fibrous products that they deserve to be mentioned. The best development of bamboo as a forest tree is in eastern China where the large species known as mao zhu, moso bamboo or hairy bamboo (*Phyllostachys edulis*) is extensively grown. It is of the running bamboo type. The stems are commonly up to 20 centimetres (12 inches) in diameter and 20 metres (66 feet) or more in height. They are used for construction poles, as well as being processed into strong laminated boards for panelling and floors. Of the clumping bamboo type, *Bambusa oldhamii* and *Bambusa vulgaris* are typical examples that attain a large size.

Asia is well endowed with flowering ornamental trees. A favourite is *Pterocarpus indicus*, variously known as angsana (Singapore), narra (Philippines), New Guinea rosewood and Solomons padauk. It is the National Tree of the Philippines, where it is popular for planting in plazas and parks, along roadsides, on school grounds, and in reafforestation projects. It is found throughout the Philippines, in natural forest usually as scattered individuals, not pure stands. Pride of India or queen's crepe myrtle (*Lagerstroemia speciosa*) has panicles of funnel-shaped, rose-pink flowers and yields a useful timber for boatbuilding. It is well known in India, Myanmar, Vietnam, Thailand and the Philippines. The State Tree of Hong Kong is the Hong Kong orchid tree (*Bauhinia* x *blakeana*). It has fragrant, rose-purple blossoms and two-lobed heart-shaped leaves. It is said that this natural hybrid of *B. variegata*, unique to southern China, was discovered near the seashore at Telegraph Bay on Hong Kong Island in the nineteenth century. It was named after Sir Henry Blake, governor of Hong Kong from 1898 to 1903, who was a strong supporter of botany. Pink shower tree (*Cassia javanica*), native to Malaysia and Indonesia, has rose-pink blossoms and is much planted as an ornamental.

Huangshan, China

Geological upwellings through the earth's crust have formed the sheer faces of granite at Huangshan in Anhui Province and pines grow perched on impossible ledges among the mountains. For centuries, poets and painters have visited Huangshan, inspired by the juxtaposition of smooth plummeting rocks and twisted trees.

It was indeed a fascinating sight, beyond imagination and quite indescribable. These pines did not grow in the soil, but on the bare rock. Their trunk and bark were stone. Nurtured by the rain and clouds, enduring snow and frost, they were conceived from the very life-essence of Nature and engendered from the depths of antiquity. They belong with the elixirs and magic mushrooms of legend and are certainly not ordinary plants.
— Qian Qianyi, *Huangshan Journal*

ABOVE: **Towada Hachimantai National Park, Japan**

The volcanic highlands and plateaux of this region of northern Honshu have long been regarded as remote and lost to the wilderness. In early medieval times, rebel nobles and exiled political reformers were banished here to roam the forests of pine and beech or to settle in the peasant homes of rural villages. Later, this mountainous region formed a natural boundary between the fiefdoms of two important shoguns. To protect 830 square kilometres (320 square miles) of forests, the region was declared a national park in 1936, one of the twelve original natural areas of Japan designated for protection. The move to establish national parks built upon age-old traditions of the veneration of nature in a country where the flowering of a tree is deemed an event worthy of a national holiday.

OPPOSITE: **Weeping willows, West Lake, Hangzhou, China**

Weeping willows are native to China, although related species are distributed across the world. The willow in China is a symbol of fragility and of lust. On the fifth day of the fifth moon, sprays of willow leaves are still hung over the doors of houses to ward off evil. The date commemorates the anniversary of an historic massacre in which families were slain by soldiers, except for certain favoured ones who left a bunch of leaves at the door.

Rokuon-ji Garden, Kyoto, Japan

An important element of Japanese gardening is *shakkei*, literally 'borrowed scenery'. A distant forested hill or a special view can be drawn into the ambience of a garden through the careful placement of certain rocks, or trees, or by 'trimming' an outlook by planting hedges or building walls. Borrowed scenery is deemed effective when it is captured alive: when distant hills, rocks or water enter the vista of the garden in all their living essence. To have a garden with merely a spectacular outlook is not considered to have 'captured' that view. Live capture of borrowed scenery takes the patience and sensitivity of a master gardener who is willing to listen to what the trees and the stones and the garden itself have to say. Japanese black pine or kuromatsu (*Pinus thunbergii)* and Japanese red pine or akamatsu (*Pinus densiflora*) are traditional conifers planted in Japanese gardens.

Oirase Valley, Japan

While around sixty percent of Japan is forested, much of this is managed for its timber, with forestry regimes favouring valuable conifers. Remnants of the original forest cover can be found in parks and in the grounds of temples where trees regarded as holy were protected. Much of Japan, from southwest Hokkaido to northern Honshu, was covered with temperate forest that featured some 168 species of trees (compared to eighty-five for the whole of Europe). Featuring in these forests still are oaks, beeches, ashes, hornbeams, maples, poplars, elms, alders, magnolias, aralias and Japanese cherry trees. Higher mountainous land is covered with dense pine and fir forests.

Tea plantation, Cameron Highlands, Malaysia

Tea comes from the *Camellia* genus of the tea family (Theaceae). The most valuable commercial species is native to north India and China. Tea has been used medicinally, socially and for pleasure for tens of centuries in China. Its active alkaloid, caffeine, and the unique taste of its infusion has built for this shrub a hallowed place in cultures around the world. Its aesthetic value was revered in this letter of AD 730 from a Chinese gentleman to a friend:

I am sending you some leaves of tea that come from a tree belonging to the Monastery of Ou I Mountain. Take a blue urn of Ni Hung and fill it with water which has been melted from snow gathered at sunrise upon the western slopes of SouChan Mountain. Place the urn over a fire of maple twigs that have just been collected from among very old moss and leave it there until the water begins to laugh. Then pour it into a cup of Huen Tscha in which you have placed some leaves of this tea. Cover the cup with a bit of white silk woven at Houa Chan and wait until your room is filled with a perfume like the garden of Fouen Lo. Lift the cup to your lips, then close your eyes. You will be in Paradise.

Maple, Hirosaki, Japan

The holy earth is overspread with leaves,
Wind crosses a thousand miles of autumn fields.
— Tesshu

The brilliant colours of the dying leaves of autumn were celebrated in ancient Japan by *momijigari*, 'hunting the autumn leaves'. These were picnics held in woodlands by nobles where the autumn colours of nature were viewed behind temporary fences of elegant silken brocade. Glimpses of views of great natural beauty were held to be divine revelations, inspiring poetry and contemplation. Japanese maple (*Acer palmatum*) has been cultivated widely by the Japanese and exists in numerous cultivars, varying in leaf shape, leaf colour, bark texture, bark, size, and growing pattern. It is used frequently in bonsai.

Japanese black pine (*Pinus thunbergii*), Yamadera, Japan

When just a few inches tall, where did you come from,
With your long life of eternal spring?
The long winds whisper poems endlessly,
As they shiver your old dragon scales.
— Monchu

ABOVE AND RIGHT: **Mountain pines, Huangshan, China**

ABOVE: **Japanese cedar (*Cryptomeria japonica*), Yamadera, Japan**

RIGHT: **Banyan fig, Singapore**

A banyan fig starts life as a germinating seed dropped by a bird or a monkey into the sunlit crown of a forest canopy tree, thus avoiding the struggle for light as a seedling in the dimness of the tropical forest floor. Down the trunk of its host, the fig sends tendrils which meet and fuse, and soon begin to wrap the tree in a deathly embrace. When these vines reach the forest floor they send the banyan's root system into the ground. The host tree is slowly strangled, and shaded, until it finally dies encased in the wooden walls of the banyan. All through the tropics, forest-dwelling people have secreted the bones of their ancestors and other treasures within the hollow hearts of banyan figs

Woods of Japanese beech (*Fagus crenata*), Oirasegawa River, Honshu, Japan

The native animistic belief of Shinto in Japan lends life to all things of nature — rivers, stones, mountains and trees. In certain mountainous regions of Japan, an old mythological creature known as a *tengu* is believed to live in the forest. Tengu, part bird/part human, live in colonies with a king. Normally hidden in the fleeting light of undisturbed forests, they may play tricks on forest travellers who lose their way.

Japanese black pine (*Pinus thunbergii*), Ginkakuji Temple, Kyoto, Japan

Oirase Valley, Honshu, Japan

In the mixed deciduous forests of Japan, a number of animals unique to this country are found. Large white-cheeked flying squirrels, the Japanese dormouse and sika deer are dependent on forest cover for survival, as are several endemic bird species.

Ginkgo tree, Hirosaki, Japan

The ginkgo, or maidenhair tree, is the sole surviving representative of a group of conifers that were widespread 200 million years ago. Then, before flowering plants had evolved, forests contained ferns, primitive conifers and cycads, and were browsed by dinosaurs. The ginkgo has survived unchanged since those times. Its archaic lobed leaves and unprotected seed are testimony to its unchanged antiquity. Its nearest relatives are found fossilised in coal seams by miners. Living ginkgos have never been found with any certainty in the wild, but they were grown in the temple gardens of China and Japan. In Japan, ginkgos are reputed to be the only plants possessing the human quality of loyalty. It is said they will die for their masters.

Coconut palms and riverhouse, Malaysia

The large buoyant seeds of the beach-fringing coconut palm float the oceans of the tropical world, bearing their watertight flasks of moisture and sustenance ready for germination on a remote shore. Where coconuts grow, people have been able to survive. The juices inside the green nut are thirst-quenching and nutritious and the dried flesh of the nut can be eaten or pressed for oil. The husks are burned for fuel, the palm fronds can be used for thatching or weaving, and the trunk is useful timber. Where there are coconut palms, there is a home for subsistence communities in the tropics.

Burmese banyan fig, Botanic Gardens, Singapore

A large fig in a tropical forest is alive with song and activity during its fruiting season. Throughout the day, streams of monkeys and birds pass through its branches, feeding on the fig's prolific fruit. Many animals centre their territories around this most productive of the trees of the tropical rainforest.

Maso-chiku bamboo forest (*Phyllostachys edulis*), Japan

Bamboo, the giant tree grass of over a thousand recorded uses, is also the fastest growing living thing in the world. On warm, moist mornings bamboo can grow at astonishing speeds, sometimes producing sounds of squeaking, whining and faint screaming as the young shoots pierce their way through the bracts and sheaths clothing the base of each culm. Bamboo occurs widely in the world but is at its most common and diverse on the continent of Asia. There are around 1000 species of bamboo, most of them flowering only at long intervals, thirty, sixty or even 120 years apart. All bamboos of the same species, wherever they are on earth, will burst into flower at exactly the same time. After flowering, the stems die. Such synchronised flowering and death causes serious problems for the endangered panda, whose diet is solely bamboo. During recent bamboo flowering in China, 140 panda were found dead in the wild from starvation.

3

THE TREES
OF AFRICA

The great continent of Africa has a distinctive and highly varied tree flora, being particularly rich in the legume family. The visitor to Kruger National Park in South Africa will come into immediate contact with mopane woodland, dominated by *Colophospermum mopane*. This tree has very hard wood and is a browse tree much favoured by elephants. Another famous African leguminous tree is Rhodesian teak (*Baikiaea plurijuga*), an important timber tree of the Kalahari Sands region of tropical Africa, also in southwest Zambia, Angola, Botswana and Zimbabwe. It is one of the finest heavy-duty timbers in the world.

The widespread open savannah with flat-topped thorny acacias and herds of grazing animals is perhaps the most uniquely African tree landscape. There are 140 or so species of African acacias (in future to be assigned to the genera *Faidherbia*, *Vachellia* and *Senegalia*). Typical representatives are camel thorn (*Acacia erioloba)* and *A. giraffe*, adapted to the hot, dry deserts of the Kalahari, and conspicuous desert shade trees; sweet thorn (*A. karroo*), a foremost acacia of southern Africa, providing nutritious fodder; paperbark acacia (*A. sieberana*); the gum arabic tree (*A. senegal*) yielding good fuelwood and a gum used in food processing and pharmaceuticals; umbrella thorn (*A. tortilis*) which favours alkaline soils; and the spectacular fever tree of the Limpopo River (*A. xanthophloea*), which grows in groups on low-lying swampy sites and has smooth, greenish-yellow bark. *Faidherbia albida* (or *Acacia albida*) thrives on river sands, and is widely distributed throughout the dry zone of Africa. It is an important component of traditional farming systems in Sahelian Africa, where it retains leaves in the dry season and sheds them in the wet (the opposite of most trees in these climates).

Southern Africa has a number of spectacular trees that are more or less just overgrown succulents. There are several tree euphorbias, such as the candelabra tree (*Euphorbia ingens*), numerous types of aloe, the largest being the aloe tree (*Aloe barberae*) which can grow as high as 20 metres (66 feet), and the bizarre halfmens plant (*Pachypodium namaquanum*), which looks from the distance like a person standing in the desert

The tropical rainforests of West Africa have long been a source of fine furniture timbers. Gaboon mahogany or okoume (*Aucoumea klaineana*) is perhaps the most important of African timbers with regard to production volume and utilisation, and is the main commercial timber tree of Gabon. It is exported to Europe, the USA, and China. Obeche (*Triplochiton scleroxylon*) is a large West African deciduous tree yielding a soft, whitish timber very popular for carpentry. From the same area, afara (*Terminalia superba*) is a large, gregarious, light-demanding, fast-growing tree with a valuable furniture timber. Wild mango, duiker nut or dika (*Irvingia gabonensis*) is a very popular and valued tree by farmers in Cameroon, the kernels of the fruit being used as a thickening agent. The mahogany family (Meliaceae) is well represented in Africa with timber trees such as African mahogany (*Khaya ivorensis*), sapele (*Entandrophragma cylindricum*), and sipo or utile (*E. utile*) being well-known examples.

Highveld protea (*Protea caffra*), Drakensberg Mountains, South Africa

LEFT: **Poinciana (Delonix regia), Rarotonga, Cook Islands, is native to Madagascar, but has been planted throughout the tropics as an ornamental tree**

BOTTOM LEFT: **Candelabra tree (Euphorbia ingens), Transvaal, South Africa**

OPPOSITE: **African tulip tree (Spathodea campanulata), Queensland, Australia, where it is introduced and has become naturalised**

The bignonia family is well represented in Africa, three examples being the sausage tree (*Kigelia pinnata*), markhamia (*Markhamia lutea*) — a tree much valued by farmers for agroforestry in Kenya, and the African tulip tree (*Spathodea campanulata*) — a striking ornamental tree with large orange-red flowers.

The trees of North Africa have affinities with those of southern Europe and the Middle East. Thus, in the Atlas Mountains of Morocco is found the Atlas cedar (*Cedrus atlantica*) and various oaks (such as *Quercus canariensis*, *Q. faginea*, *Q. pyrenaica*). An unusual conifer of the cypress family, *Tetraclinis articulata*, is also found here. Argan tree, Moroccan ironwood (*Argania spinosa*), is a spiny, normally evergreen tree of the Sapotaceae family. The species is endemic in Morocco and is one of the most remarkable trees in North Africa for its ecology and for its social value as a multipurpose tree. The main products are the fruits and the leaves, for the production of oil and as forage. Argan covers an area of about 8200 square kilometres (3166 square miles), forming a typical forest region in the southwest of Morocco. The species was probably already known to the Phoenicians in the tenth century BC, and methods for the extraction of the oil are described in a medical book of the thirteenth century.

Conifers are not particularly prominent in southern Africa, the best known being South Africa's National Tree, real yellowwood (*Podocarpus latifolius*), which is esteemed for furniture wood making, and the Mulanje cedar (*Widdringtonia whytei*), Malawi's National Tree, and a large one, to 40 metres (131 feet) tall, giving an excellent construction timber.

Mention must be made of the baobab. African baobab or monkey breadfruit (*Adansonia digitata*) is said to live well over 2000 years. It is a deciduous tree up to 15 metres (49 feet) tall, but the diameter of the bole can reach an enormous 8 metres (26 feet). Baobabs are also found in Madagascar, where there are seven species. Madagascar parted company with Africa some 120 million years ago, and has been isolated so long that around eighty percent of the trees there are endemic. Some famous trees from here are the flamboyant poinciana (*Delonix regia*), planted throughout the tropics as an ornamental; the triangle palm (*Dypsis decaryi*); the peculiar, spiny octopus tree (*Alluaudia ascendens* and *A. procera*) with tall stems covered in thorns along their entire length, and *Didierea madagascariensis* with a short trunk and several upright stems.

Sausage tree (Kigelia pinnata), Kenya

The sausage tree is semi-deciduous and capable of reaching heights of 25 metres (80 feet). It is a member of the bignonia family, which is well represented in Africa.

Fever tree (*Acacia xanthophloea*), Kenya

The acacia is the quintessential African savannah tree. The spreading open branches that comprise its distinctive shape are a distinguishing feature of the grasslands. There are many species, each with differing requirements for soil or for water availability, enabling the genus *Acacia* to fill many different niches across Africa. Acacias have evolved a number of adaptations to withstand the hot, dry conditions of the open savannah. These include small leaves and a deep rooting system. Even their rate of photosynthesis is adapted to function most efficiently at high temperatures. Based on the general appearance of their flowers, the African acacias are divided into two groups. One, which includes the fever tree, has bright pompom flowers. The other group has long flowers resembling bottlebrushes.

Zambezi River Gorge, Zambia

Across the river, near our sacred grove
Where the leopard roars
— Su-dom: Akan funeral dirges

Certain groves of trees and forests in many parts of Africa are set apart from everyday use. They are made sacred by their association with religious ceremonies, rituals and sacrifices. In these groves there can be no grazing, cropping or fuelwood gathering. If animals or people hide there, they may not be pursued as the grove confers sanctuary, guarded by the wrath of God or by spirits.

ABOVE: **Victoria Falls, Zimbabwe**

A deep crack in the earth crosses the path of the Zambezi River at the Victoria Falls, sending the river plunging 108 metres (355 feet) into a long canyon. In the rainy season, spray from this 1370 metre (4500 feet) wide waterfall rises far above the falls, and can be seen for many kilometres, giving meaning to the Makololo name for the Victoria Falls, Mosi-oa-a-tunya ('the smoke that thunders'). Spray falls as a constant light rain along the canyon's edges, creating a rainforest in miniature, complete with moisture-loving epiphytes, ferns and palms, and lush ground plants. Beyond the reaches of the localized rains, vegetation quickly returns to scrubby dry woodlands and the soil to sand. Over the eons, the Victoria Falls have been retreating upriver as the Zambezi cuts further and further into the weak faults of its black basalt riverbed. The past progression of this process can be measured by some 100 kilometres (62 miles) of deep gorges that zigzag beside the river below the falls. As the waterfall retreats over time, so the tiny spray forest will follow its creator up the river.

Fig tree (*Ficus natalensis*) encircling Natal mahogany (*Trichilia emetica*), Ndumo, South Africa

This widely distributed tree, also known as the common wild fig, is sacred to local tribespeople in some areas. In season, pigeons and starlings flock to eat the fruit.

Fever trees, Ndumo Reserve, South Africa

The Latin name for the fever tree is *Acacia xanthophloea*. 'Xanthophloea' means 'yellow bark' and it was this distinctive feature of the riverside acacias that the early European settlers to Africa believed was the cause of malaria. Fever trees grow only along rivers and near pools where malaria is most common. It was only later that it was discovered that mosquitoes (which breed in water) carry malaria and that the fever tree was innocent.

Umbrella thorn tree, Natal, South Africa

The umbrella thorn, or paperbark acacia (*Acacia sieberana*), is a widespread acacia found in tropical Africa from Senegal to Ethiopia and south to the Transvaal and Natal. Its bark is corky and this is thought to provide an insulation against the damaging effect of the fires which spread through its wooded grassland habitat in the dry season.

Camel thorn tree, Namib Desert, Namibia

Rain never falls in the Namib. The surprising diversity of life which manages to survive in these red sands depends for moisture on fog, which rolls in from the sea and bathes the desert one day out of five, or on deep underground rivers, as does the camel thorn (*Acacia erioloba*).

Marula trees, Northern Transvaal, South Africa

The fruit of the marula (*Sclerocarya birrea*) is so highly prized these trees are protected under tribal law and are customarily left standing when fields are cleared in southern Africa. Marula is in the mango family — a relationship revealed by its delicious fruit that is eaten eagerly by both people and animals. A liqueur, 'Amarula', is made from the fruit. The tree's uses, which extend to its soft, light wood (for carving bowls, pestles and stools) include magic. It is believed to be a tree of fertility, able to control the sex of unborn babies.

Bamboo, Bulawayo, Zimbabwe

This is the highly ornamental golden vivax bamboo
(*Phyllostachys vivax* 'Aureocaulis'), originating
in eastern China.

Camel thorn tree, Namib Desert, Namibia

The camel thorn is a desert tree of great
importance, bearing fruit and flowers and
providing wood and shade where all such
commodities are rare.

Baobab tree, Messina, South Africa

Always
Is calm;
Be it dry
Or rainy season,
Water is never scarce
Within
— Yoruba praise song

The baobab (*Adansonia digitata*) is a memorable tree, with its shining smooth grey bark and wildly arranged bare branches. It has adapted to the dry lands it inhabits by storing water in the fibrous sponge of its enormous bulk of soft wood. The baobab drops its leaves through long droughts and waits like a dead tree for life-bringing rains. Large baobabs can be ancient. Some have been carbon-dated to an age of 2000 years. They grow slowly.

Rock fig, Swaziland

The common name for the rock fig (*Ficus ingens*) is drawn from its muscular roots which can split rocks. Figs are of immense ecological importance in their habitat, with their fruit providing food for a great number of birds and other dependent animals.

Sycamore fig, Transvaal, South Africa

The survival of these large sycamore figs (*Ficus sycamorus)* is, like all figs, dependent on a tiny wasp. Without the wasp, the fig would not have its flowers pollinated and so could not reproduce. Flowers of figs are hidden in a closed receptacle that looks like a fruit from the outside. At the tip of the 'fruit' is a small opening which admits a tiny fig wasp whose task it is to pollinate the flowers. A female wasp enters the fig 'fruit' to lay her eggs in special sterile flowers that the fig produces for this purpose. In doing so, she transfers pollen to adjacent fertile flowers from the fig that was her birthplace. Male wasps enter the fruit to inseminate her daughters while they lie unhatched in the sterile brood flowers. The fig tree times the maturity of its male, pollen-producing flowers to the hatching of the female wasp so that their pollen will be carried away on her as she leaves to lay her own eggs in a new fig. Everything about the reproductive biology of figs and fig wasps is thus interrelated, indicating a long evolutionary association between these plants and their insect pollinators. Should the tiny wasp vanish, so too would the fig.

Baobab tree, Zimbabwe

Baobabs have innumerable uses to the people of the dry lands in which they grow. Their spongy wood can be macerated to make rope or paper. The leaves and pollen are eaten. Their seeds are refreshing to suck or they may be roasted and ground to make coffee. The fruit pod contains tartaric acid, so the baobab is often called 'the cream-of-tartar' tree.

Tribal people in Africa have sought explanations for the strange form of this important tree which grows in their dry lands. Common to many legends is a story that God, in a fit of anger because the baobab could not decide which habitat to settle in, threw the tree over his shoulder. It landed on its crown and has grown, roots upward, ever since. Small baobabs look so different from their parents — small nondescript shrubs — that even the San, who know these lands so intimately, believe that the baobab does not grow from these shrubs. They say these trees come fully grown and the dull thumps of their crashing to the earth can be heard frequently in the peace of the wide desert lands.

Acacia tree, savannah landscape, Kenya

The 140 or so species of African acacias, perfectly adapted to the flat, dry landscapes they inhabit, play a vital role in local ecosystems and economies.

Halfmens plant, Hester Malan Nature Reserve, South Africa

Among us grows a palm, with a hairy chest
Among us grows a strange tree, coiffed like
a statue
— Tshimini, Luba clan praise song

Long ago the Khoisan Nama left their homelands and migrated south, with the injunction never to look back. There were some that could not resist a last longing look towards their beloved homelands and those people were at once turned to 'half men' with their heads of leafy rosettes facing the northern sun. Halfmens (*Pachypodium namaquanum*), honoured by the Nama as their ancestors, live in the harsh rocky lands fringing the Namib Desert. They germinate in a storm of rain and send down a root in the first twenty-four hours of growth. There they may wait, hardly growing for twenty-four months, or even twenty-four years, until the rains come again. Bursts of rain trigger synchronised growth among halfmens, so they are often found in single-age stands — poised ghosts looking to their ancient northern homeland.

Silver tree, Kirstenbosch Botanical Gardens, Cape Town, South Africa

The silver tree (*Leucadendron argenteum*) occurs naturally only on Table Mountain, Cape Town, South Africa.

Dragon tree (*Dracaena hookeriana*), Kenya

This attractive evergreen shrub has long, strap-like leaves. Many members of the widely-distributed Dracaena family are prized as ornamentals.

ABOVE: **Savannah at sunset, Kenya**

LEFT: **Camel thorn tree and weaverbird nests, Namibia**

Numerous, the weaverbirds
The gray ones that go about in swarms
Children with the little red beaks
Children making a noise in the mimosa tree
— Sotho animal praise song

There are around eighty-five species of weaverbirds in Africa. They weave beautifully intricate nests from the grasses of the African savannahs. Many nests incorporate protective devices to keep out predators. They may be constructed on branches overhanging water, have tunnel entrances, or be placed in association with nests of stinging wasps. Social weavers build spectacularly large communal nests which hang like huge dark sacks from their acacia hosts.

Quiver trees, Kokerboom Forest, Namibia

Living in the company of other trees of bizarre and wondrous form, the quiver tree (*Aloe dichotoma*) is restricted to the very arid areas of Namaqualand and southern Namibia. The San used its fibrous core to make arrow quivers and so gave the tree its common name. It is a strictly protected tree in South Africa.

4

THE TREES OF NORTH AMERICA

It is convenient to begin the North American tree journey in the Pacific Northwest – the home of giant conifers unparalleled anywhere else in the world. The seaward slopes of the Cascade Ranges are moist and mild, and the volcanic soils support luxuriant tree growth. Sitka spruce (*Picea sitchensis*) grows to a huge size in the almost rainforest conditions of the Olympic Peninsula, and Douglas fir (*Pseudotsuga menziesii*), grand fir (*Abies grandis*), Pacific silver fir (*A. amabilis*), western hemlock (*Tsuga heterophylla*), western red cedar (*Thuja plicata*) and western white pine (*Pinus monticola*) complete an impressive line-up of massive conifers, all of which are important timber trees. Broadleaved trees here play only a secondary role, with big-leaved maple (*Acer grandidentata*), red alder (*Alnus rubra*), Oregon ash (*Fraxinus latifolia*), black cottonwood (*Populus trichocarpa*), and the evergreen Pacific madrone (*Arbutus menziesii*) being the main examples. Southwards near the coast will be encountered shore pine (a subspecies of *Pinus contorta*), the huge sugar pine (*Pinus lambertiana*), the California laurel (*Umbellularia californica*) — an unusual evergreen sometimes called the headache tree — and tan oak (*Lithocarpus densiflorus*).

California boasts some of the world's great trees, pride of place going to the two kinds of redwoods – the coast redwood (*Sequoia sempervirens*) and the Sierra redwood or giant sequoia (*Sequoiadendron giganteum*). Just north of San Francisco, in an isolated canyon, grows the ancient coast redwood forest known the world over as Muir Woods. These 1000-year-old giant trees, towering 80–90 metres (260–300 feet) high, moved the famed naturalist John Muir to call this '...the best tree-lovers monument that could possibly be found in all the forests of the world.' Sierra redwood grows in some 72 small groves at 900–2200 metres (3000–7000 feet), in the Sierra Nevada Mountains, and may attain an age of more than 3500 years. These trees are the world's largest living organisms, regularly attaining 2000 tonnes in weight. 'General Sherman' is the biggest of the giant trees; it is estimated to weigh 6000 tonnes.

Aspens, Nevada

Aspens provide a year-round food supply for many forest animals. Both snowshoe hares and cottontail rabbits nibble the branches where they swing low to the ground. Moose, porcupines and white-tailed deer browse it, surviving the winter on what nutrition they can draw from the twigs. Birds such as grosbeaks and purple finches eat the buds or nest in its hollows. Aspen is important, too, to beavers, who eat many parts of the tree but depend mostly on the bark of the young uppermost limbs. Beavers chew down whole trees to reach these and will store them in mud on the bottom of their dammed lakes through the winter. When summer arrives, the distinguishing feature of the aspen is the unceasing shiver of its leaves as these turn and rustle on their long petioles in the slightest breeze. Onondage Indians called the tree 'nut-hi-e' or 'noisy leaf'. They used its brewed bark in a bitter drink to treat coughs.

Vermont

The North American deciduous forests support many more species than those of Europe and west Asia. A significant contributing factor for this enhanced diversity is probably the orientation of the main mountain ranges. In Europe, they run west-east across the continent, creating a barrier of snowy peaks and cool montane slopes. That barrier would have been difficult for warmth-loving plants to cross from the south after the last glaciation had caused their extinction in the cold north. In North America, the principal mountain ranges run north-south, leaving pathways for recolonisation after the glaciers retreated.

Further inland is found another of America's great conifers, the ponderosa pine (*Pinus ponderosa*). It grows in the Coast Ranges too, but is at its best in the Sierra Nevada. The Rocky Mountains of Canada and the United States share the beautiful spire-like Englemann spruce (*Picea engelmannii*) and subalpine fir (*Abies lasiocarpa*), lodgepole pine (*Pinus contorta*), and also the attractively-barked quaking aspen (*Populus tremuloides*) and paper birch (*Betula papyrifera*). The northernmost forests of North America, stretching across Canada, are dominated by jack pine (*Pinus banksiana*), tamarack (*Larix laricina*), black spruce (*Picea mariana*), white spruce (*Picea glauca*), and balsam fir (*Abies balsamea*), along with aspen, birch, and various willows.

The trees of the eastern and southern states of the USA are much more diverse than those in the west, but not of such imposing dimensions. It is a region of pine woods and mixed deciduous broadleaved forests, with a tropical extension in southern Florida. While white pine (*Pinus strobus*) is a feature of the northeast, it is loblolly pine (*P. taeda*) that is highly characteristic of the southeast and is the mainstay of the pulp and paper industry. It grows both on the coastal plains and rolling piedmont country, with a great capacity to invade and colonise old abandoned fields. Slash pine (*P. elliottii*) and longleaf pine (*P. palustris*) are the main pine-wood trees of Florida and the Gulf states, and were at one time tapped for resin. The deciduous swamp cypress (*Taxodium distichum*) is a feature of coastal inlets and swamps, and it is often accompanied by water tupelo (*Nyssa aquatica*).

The southern mixed hardwood forest of the USA is North America's richest tree ecosystem. The variety of trees is impressive. The walnut family is very well represented, with the black walnut (*Juglans nigra*) — an esteemed cabinet timber — butternut (*J. cinerea*), shagbark hickory (*Carya ovata*), and pecan (*Carya illinoinensis*) being examples. Hickory wood is renowned for making the best axe handles, while pecan has the finest edible nut.

Oaks comprise the biggest southern tree group, being unrivalled for their economic importance as timber and pulpwood. Live oak (*Quercus virginiana*) is a rather special species as it is evergreen, grows near the coast, and is commonly festooned with 'Spanish moss' – a kind of pendant epiphytic bromeliad. The white oak group have leaves with rounded lobes, the white oak (*Q. alba*) and bur oak (*Q. macrocarpa*) being examples. The red oaks are more numerous and are distinguished by their bristle-tipped, deeply lobed leaves; examples are southern red oak (*Q. falcata*), northern red oak (*Q. rubra*), Shumard oak (*Q. shumardii*), pin oak (*Q. palustris*), and scarlet oak (*Q. coccinea*).

The so-called bottomlands — the fertile river banks of the southern rivers — have sycamore (*Platanus occidentalis*), boxelder maple (*Acer negundo*), red maple (*A. rubrum*), sweet gum (*Liquidambar styraciflua*), southern magnolia (*Magnolia grandiflora*), and black tupelo (*Nyssa sylvatica*). The forests of the Appalachian Mountains are very rich in trees, which include the tulip tree (*Liriodendron tulipifera*), black locust (*Robinia pseudoacacia*), white basswood (*Tilia heterophylla*), eastern hemlock (*Tsuga canadensis*), and eastern white pine (*Pinus strobus*), this latter being very prone to suffering from atmospheric pollution.

One of the scenic glories of the world is the fall colour display in the New England states of the northeast. Vermont claims to have the most ideal combination of soil conditions, tree species and climate to give the best array of coloured fall foliage, but the whole region including New York State, and down into the Appalachians can be similarly spectacular. Mid September to mid October is the time to see the colours at their best, though some years are better than others. Experts believe that global warming has diminished the intensity of the colours in recent times. At the onset of fall, some leaves turn yellow, others orange, and others a brilliant red. The yellow-leaved species include green ash (*Fraxinus pennsylvanica*), aspen (*Populus tremuloides*), beech (*Fagus grandifolia*), birch (*Betula papyrifera*) and tamarack (*Larix laricina*). The red species are sugar maple (*Acer saccharum*), red maple (*A. rubrum*) and various oaks (*Quercus alba*, *Q. coccinea*, *Q. palustris*). Red maple is responsible for the most brilliant red colour, while sugar maple produces a more muted orange or gold.

Southern Quebec

Wetlands sheltered by forest provide vulnerable animals with a diverse habitat where they may feed and hide. The stability of the fragile wetland itself is also protected by surrounding trees which shield the soil from eroding rains and stabilise the water table.

ABOVE: **Vermont**

Each autumn, New England is flooded with visitors who come to witness the autumn colours of the deciduous forest — a natural spectacle of colour that is announced, as it emerges across the landscape, by radio stations and daily newspaper reports. Local communities have built livelihoods from this pilgrimage, benefiting from a national reverence for the beauty of trees.

OPPOSITE: **Maples, Maine**

There are thirteen maple species native to North America and most are concentrated in the eastern half of the continent. In spring, before the first flush of leaf growth, there is a burst of unseen activity as the tree sends sugars stored during the previous summer up the trunk, out along the branches to the twigs and leaf buds, to provide energy for the bud burst. In the sugar maple, the pressure of the sugary sap rising beneath the bark can be substantial. Maple-sugar farmers tap the rising sap with metal spikes hammered into the bark. Indians knew the sweet sap and tapped the maples for generations. Small forest animals, like squirrels, also relish the sap, chewing holes in the branches and licking up the sweet exudate.

ABOVE: **Paper birch (*Betula papyrifera*), Quebec, Canada**

Along with the equally attractive quaking aspen (*Populus tremuloides*), these birches are found on the slopes of the Rocky Mountains in both Canada and the United States.

LEFT: **Smuggler's Notch, Vermont**

Smuggler's Notch is a narrow mountain pass with 300-metre (1000-foot) cliffs either side. At one time, the only access was by footpath and riding trail. In the early part of the 19th century, when trade with Canada and great Britain was outlawed, people from Vermont carried goods through Smuggler's Notch. Later, fugitive slaves escaped to Canada through the notch, and liquor was brought south during the Prohibition era of the 1920s. There are many unique and endangered species of plants growing in Smuggler's Notch. These are alpine species that thrive on the cold damp rocky walls.

Coast redwoods, California

The coast redwood or Californian redwood (*Sequoia sempervirens*), the tallest tree in the world, builds a forest of close-growing giants in a narrow belt alongside the Pacific Ocean where morning sea fog regularly envelops the land in a warm, eerie dampness. For more than two millennia a single tree may grow here, spiralling in its deeply fissured russet-red bark to reach a height of close to 100 metres (328 feet). The largest trees, growing so closely together that barely a path can be found between them, are found on the alluvial flats. Here, rivers emerge from the coastal mountains laden with enriching silt. When these rivers flood and dump deep layers of nutrient-rich silt over the forest floor, the redwoods simply form new root mats to access these nutrients and send their trunks higher still. The name of this and other sequoias commemorates the Indian chief Sequoyah, who is famed for devising an eighty-three-letter alphabet for the Cherokee language.

Giant sequoia, Yosemite National Park, California

High on the western slopes of the Sierra Nevada in isolated forest groves grow the massive-boled giant sequoias (*Sequoiadendron giganteum*), also know as Sierra redwoods. They are among the world's largest trees. Over the 3000 or more years that they may survive, their colossal trunks can attain more than 30 metres (100 feet) in circumference and grow nearly 90 metres (295 feet) in height. Giant sequoias are wrapped in a protective, fire-resistant padding of soft bark, up to 60 centimetres (23 inches) thick, inside which they are insulated from forest fires which would kill off most other trees. Despite their antiquity and rarity, giant sequoias were targeted by loggers. Madison Grant, president of the New York Zoological Society and one of the founders of the Save the Redwoods League, wrote in 1918: 'It is scarcely necessary to dwell on the crime involved in the destruction of the oldest trees on earth. The cutting of a sequoia for grape stakes or railroad ties is like ... lighting one's pipe with a Greek manuscript to save the trouble of reaching for one's matches.'

Swamp cypresses, Atchafalaya Basin, Louisiana

The southern rivers of Louisiana and Florida meander through flooded swamplands in the watery world of the bayou. One tree has adapted most successfully to this semi-submerged habitat — the ancient swamp cypress (*Taxodium distichum*). Also known as the bald cypress (because it is leafless in the winter), this tree has developed knee roots which rise above the level of the waters. These contain spongy tissue which absorbs oxygen, allowing the root system to survive in the often stagnant water of the bayou. The seeds of the swamp cypress need waterlogged soil to germinate, and the tree's wood is almost impervious to rot. Swamp cypresses grow to a great height and can be long lived — one was recorded as having grown for 1300 years. The great age of the cypresses seems accentuated by their grey beards of Spanish moss which drift among their branches and tangle around their leaves. Spanish moss (*Tillandsia usneoides*) is a bizarre relative of the pineapple. It depends on the host cypress only for a place to hang — it does not penetrate and feed from the tree. The Indian tribes of Louisiana say that Spanish moss is the hair of a bride who was murdered at her wedding by an enemy tribe. In their grief, her family hung her long hair over the cypress branches where in time it turned grey and blew through the bayous on the wind.

Live oak, Jefferson Island, Louisiana

The live oak (*Quercus virginiana*) is synonymous with the deep south of the United States, where plantation owners often planted it for its grace and shade on their mansion lawns. The name comes from the fact that this oak does not lose its leaves in the winter and appear dead in that season, as do other oaks. Warm winter months in the south mean that the live oak can keep its leaves year round. The first National Forest Reserve in the United States was established to protect a forest of live oak (in Florida in 1828). Live oak had proved itself by then as a strong hull timber on the ship named *Constitution* or 'Old Ironsides'. So strong was the hull, that cannonballs were said to roll off it like water off a duck's back. President John Quincy Adams attempted to limit the frenzy of live oak felling that followed this discovery by establishing the reserve, but need and greed quickly overcame the conservation sentiment and the reserve was disestablished and its trees felled only five years after it was set aside. Spanish moss characteristically drapes the branches.

Grand Canyon, Arizona

The Grand Canyon is 365 kilometres (227 miles) long, 1.6 kilometres (1 mile) deep and as much as 29 kilometres (18 miles) wide. This wide, deep gash across the southwestern drylands is totally unbridgeable for many animals, particularly the abert and kaibab squirrels. The story of these squirrels is also a story of trees. The two squirrels were once the same species, entirely dependent for survival on ponderosa pine (*Pinus ponderosa*). During the last ice ages the climate of the region was cool and moist enough to allow the growth of ponderosa pine right around the canyon and into its deep interior. Through all this forest, the squirrels ranged. As the ice retreated, the climate gradually became drier and suitable habitat for the ponderosa shrank until the pines formed two distinct forests — one on the south rim of the canyon and one on the north. In each forest, a squirrel population was trapped and, isolated over time, these evolved into separate species.

Piñon pine, Grand Canyon, Arizona

The piñon pine (*Pinus edulis*) yields a nutritious seed which was of such importance to the Great Basin Indians that many clans built their lives around its cycle of productivity. Piñon seeds were eaten raw or roasted, ground into flour, or mashed as nut butter. In the southwest, the Navajos boiled resin from the piñon pine with sheep and goat hooves to make a glue for their turquoise and silver jewellery. It also made a non-stick surface on their stone pans, used for cooking corn bread. The Hopi mixed the resin with leaves and clay to create an inky dye for their wool and they smeared it over their woven baskets to make waterbearing containers. They believed that they could be protected from sorcerers by applying the resin to their foreheads.

ABOVE: **Engelmann spruce (*Picea engelmannii*), Great Basin National Park, Nevada**

Scientists are beginning to use the descriptive terms from the indigenous languages of North America to distinguish the different forms of snow. The term 'qali', for example, is a word used for 'snow on trees'. As snow piles deeply on branches in the still forest, the weight may eventually cause them to bend and then to break. In spring and summer, the loss of those branches allows more light to penetrate the forest, thus affecting the germination and growth of light-dependent seedlings on the forest floor.

RIGHT: **Bristlecone pine, Wheeler Peak, Nevada**

Bristlecone pines (*Pinus aristata*) are the oldest living things on earth. The oldest bristlecone has been dated at over 4500 years: 1000 years older than Stonehenge and 3700 years older than Westminster Abbey. That tree is still growing. Most of its oldest parts have died but its life continues in a rim of living cells that remain under a narrow strip of bark. Bristlecone pines grow in the mountains of the southwestern United States but achieve their greatest longevity in the White Mountains, where little rain falls and the soil is more rock than earth. From studying the rings of its stone-slow growth, researchers have built a picture of regional climate change, of rain and drought patterns, over thousands of years.

ABOVE: **Zion National Park, Utah**

This park encompasses 607 square kilometres (234 square miles) of wilderness canyon country. Large numbers of visitors come to see the sheer red and white cliffs of Zion Canyon, along with the many other unique geological features offered by the park.

OPPOSITE: **Joshua tree (*Yucca brevifolia*), Mojave Desert, California**

The yuccas are monocotyledons related to the agaves (*Agave*) and furcraeas (*Furcraea*), each species being pollinated by a particular species of moth. The Joshua tree is evergreen, with sharp blue-green leaves clustered at the end of branches. It is one of the most characteristic of Mojave Desert plants, named by Mormon pioneers for the Biblical hero raising his arms to heaven.

**Ponderosa pine (*Pinus ponderosa*),
Zion National Park, Utah**

The ponderosa pine is one of the most widely
distributed of all the native North American
pines. It has a very deep tap root which can
reach far into the earth in search of water,
ensuring its survival where other trees fail.

ABOVE: **Alder tree, Vermont**

Mature trees the size of this alder may have hundreds of thousands of leaves. The average mature oak, for example, has 700,000 leaves. These are not arranged randomly on the tree. Along with the branches and twigs, leaves are positioned at precise intervals and consistent angles to maximise the interception of sunlight. In this way, the tree presents the maximum surface area to the energy-giving sunlight.

LEFT: **Monterey cypress, Point Lobos, California**

The Monterey cypress (*Cupressus macrocarpa*) is native to very small areas of sea cliff at Point Lobos and Cypress Point near Monterey, California. Its windswept and tortured form embodies the salt winds and sea storms that the trees must endure along this exposed coast. Seeds from these few trees have been collected and planted all around the world, generating hedges, shelter belts and timber forests. In better sites, Monterey cypress readily grows to great heights.

Central Park, New York

That the heart of New York City has been dedicated to a park of trees demonstrates the high value placed on the presence of trees in the midst of one of the greatest concentrations of buildings, technology and people on earth. People can leave behind many aspects of nature when they move to cities, but it seems trees are not among them. The trees of Central Park have citizens groups especially established to defend and care for them.

5

THE TREES
OF SOUTH AMERICA

South America (including Central America and the West Indies) is immensely rich in tree species. The region is a stronghold of leguminous trees and several of them have become popular ornamentals throughout the tropics and subtropics. One of the best known and admired trees from this region is the rain tree or monkey pod (*Samanea saman*). It originates from Central America but has been planted throughout the tropics as a shade tree. It can be seen to perfection in Singapore; in the streets of Lautoka, Fiji; at Mossman, Queeensland, Australia; and in Hawaii.

From Brazil comes the leopard tree (*Caesalpinia ferrea*), a tree with attractive, smoothly mottled bark, much planted in the streets of Brisbane, Australia. Brazil's National Tree – pau brasil (*Caesalpinia echinata*) is also a member of the legume family. The country is named after this tree, one that is famous for its beautiful red wood. However, the most prized of all Brazilian woods is jacarandá or Brazilian rosewood (*Dalbergia nigra*). The tipa tree or pride of Bolivia (*Tipuana tipu*) hails from Bolivia and northwest Argentina, and with its spreading crown and yellow flowers, makes a fine shade tree. Argentina and Uruguay share the same National Tree – ceibo (*Erythrina crista-galli*), a deciduous legume with spectacular red flowers. In the Caribbean carib wood or sabinea (*Poitea carinalis*) is a small deciduous tree, nominated as the Dominican Republic's National Tree on account of its brilliant red flowers.

The bignonia family is another highly characteristic feature of Central and South America, containing numerous highly valuable trees, both for amenity and timber. National Trees feature prominently in this group too, with lapacho (*Tabebuia heptaphylla*) being Paraguay's chosen tree, Venezuela's the araguana (*T. chrysantha*), and the yellow trumpet flower (*T. chrysotricha,*) which is the official flower of Brazil. From northwest Argentina comes the popular and attractive *Jacaranda mimosifolia*, much planted in avenues in many cities of the world, such as Pretoria in South Africa and Tunis in Tunisia.

The bombax family has a number of spectacular trees. The silk kapok tree (*Ceiba pentandra*) of the West Indies and Central America was formerly the main plywood species of Iquitos area (Peru), but the resource is now much depleted. Kapok is floss from the inner capsule wall and was once much used in lifebelts, lifejackets, mattresses, pillows, upholstery, saddles and sleeping bags. It is eight times as light as cotton, has low thermal conductivity, and is an excellent sound absorber. The floss-silk tree (*Chorisia speciosa*) of Brazil and Argentina has spines on the trunk and branches. Maga (*Montezuma speciosissima*) is the National Tree of Puerto Rico, where it is cultivated as a street tree. Balsa *(Ochroma pyramidale)* of Central America, the West Indies, and South America, is a fast-growing evergreen tree with exceedingly lightweight wood. Pochote (*Pachira quinata*), also known as *Bombacopsis quinata,* is a spiny-stemmed deciduous tree of Central and South America, which also provides useful lightweight utility timber.

Lake Conguillio, Chile

Deep valleys and steep slopes, covered with auracarias and beech forest, show great scars caused by lava flows. The lake was formed when the drainage of the Sierra Nevada range was blocked by these flows several hundred years ago, and the standing trunks of trees can still be seen under the clear waters of the lake.

Mexico is rich in temperate and tropical forests which contain the highest number of pine and oak species anywhere in the world. They often grow together in mixed forests. In northern Mexico durango pine (*Pinus durangensis*) is commercially the most important. Central America and the West Indies also have coniferous forests, examples being the three varieties of the Caribbean pine – *P. caribaea* var. *caribaea* being from Cuba, *P. caribaea* var. *bahamensis* from the Bahamas, and *P. caribaea* var. *hondurensis* from Belize, Nicaragua, Honduras and Guatemala. This tropical pine has succeeded well in plantations in many parts of the world. Other notable Mexican trees include mahogany, zapote and ceiba (also known as pochote), the sacred tree of the Maya. Mexico's National Tree is a conifer – the Mexican bald cypress or ahuehuete (*Taxodium mucronatum*), which thrives along rivers and creeks in the semi-arid regions. Near Oaxaca, in the town of Tulé, is the famed giant cypress now thought to be at least 2000 years old. According to legend, Hernán Cortés cried beneath the boughs of a bald cypress after the Aztecs defeated the Spanish on La Noche Triste (The Sad Night).

There are two main kinds of mahogany. Broadleaved or Honduran mahogany (*Swietenia macrophylla*) is indigenous to the Central American countries, and extends into northern South America, particularly Brazil, Bolivia, Peru, Venezuela, Colombia, and French Guiana. This is the Central American mahogany of commerce, and is still important today in the international timber trade. The other one is narrow-leaved or Cuban mahogany (*S. mahagoni*), which is also found in Florida, USA. The timber is famous for furniture and boatbuilding.

Chile and Argentina at the southern end of the continent share several trees of the so-called Gondwana flora. Among the most abundant are the southern beeches such as roble (*Nothofagus obliqua*), coigüe (*N. dombeyi*), lenga (*N. pumilio*) and rauli (*N. procera*). There are conifers in the southern Andes forests as well, notably Chilean cedar (*Austrocedrus chilensis*), alerce (*Fitzroya cupressoides*), and the famed monkey puzzle tree (*Araucaria araucana*). Southern Brazil also has conifers, the best known being parana pine (*A. angustifolia*).

The Amazon region of Brazil and Peru contains several thousand species of tree. The Brazil nut or castanha-do-Pará tree (*Bertholletia excelsa*) is one of the most important economic plant species of Amazonia. Brazil nuts are mostly collected during the five to six months of the rainy season and together with rubber, which is tapped during the dry season, provide year-round income to forest dwellers. These two products are often cited as the most important of the extractive reserves in Amazonia. The rubber tree (*Hevea brasiliensis*) belongs to the euphorbia family. It is now grown most extensively in southern Asia. Another economic plant, quinine (*Cinchona calisaya*), is the National Tree of Peru, the bark of which contains alkaloids much used at one time against malaria.

Palms are abundant in Central and South America. Colombia's National Tree is the wax palm (*Ceroxylon quindiuense*), which at 70 metres (230 feet) is the world's tallest palm. Cuba's National Tree is also a palm, the royal palm (*Roystonea regia*), a feature of parks and botanical gardens throughout the tropics. The pindó or queen palm (*Syagrus romanzoffiana*) is much cultivated in the subtropics and grows naturally beside the imposing Iguassú Falls in Argentina and Brazil.

OPPOSITE: **Queen palm (*Syagrus romanzoffiana*), Iguassu Falls, Argentina**

ABOVE: **Southern beech (*Nothofagus*) forest, Lake District, Chile**

There are nine species of southern beech (*Nothofagus*) in Chile, each adapted to a slightly different forest niche. The beech species mingle and change as soils, moisture and temperature change down the length of Chile and up the slopes of the Andes. Several species are deciduous, and these are found in the cooler zones, one forming the tree line where forest gives way to alpine meadows.

Conguillio National Park, Chile

Conguillio means 'water with feathers' in the Araucanian language. Among the greatest attractions of the park is the Llaima volcano, 3125 metres (10,250 feet), its lakes and lagoons of volcanic origin, and the ancient araucaria forests, many of which are unexplored. This park is also known as 'the umbrellas', due to the characteristic shape of the trees.

Beech, Lake District, Chile

And I came to the fields and wide places of memory
— St Augustine

Cleared fields interspersed with stands of native forest are a common pattern of farmed land in central Chile and the Lake District. The only access to many farms is by horseback along forest tracks or by boat across the numerous lakes of the region. Pioneering in these lands had left large tracts of indigenous forest intact, but these are now being logged at an increasing rate.

Araucaria, Llaima Volcano, Chile

The perfect geometry of their prickly branches
signals the archaic origins of the araucarias
(*Araucaria araucana*), known in their native
Chile as umbrella trees and around the world as
Chilean monkey-puzzles. Mesozoic forests 200
million years ago were rich in such primitive
conifers, along with cycads, gingkos and
ferns. Araucarias can be found today growing
on ridge crests or other difficult sites on the
western slopes and valleys of the Andes and
on the parallel ridges of the coastal cordillera.
Their distinctive umbrella silhouettes against
symmetrical volcanoes epitomise the landscapes
of central Chile.

ABOVE: **Pines, Chile**

RIGHT: **Old man's beard lichen (*Usnea*) on the bark of monkey puzzle trees (*Araucaria araucana*), Chile**

Araucaria trees, Lonquimay Volcano, Chile

The name araucaria, which has been given to the whole family of these distinctive conifers, is taken from the Araucarian Indians who lived in the forests of central and southern Chile. They were courageous fighters who earned the respect of the invading Spanish for their fierce defence of their forest homelands. The Araucarian Indians' staple food was the seed of the araucaria tree. They migrated between araucaria forests at the end of summer to gather the date-sized seeds. These seeds were roasted in hot ashes, or cooked in meat stews, or they were strung on threads of sinew to dry by the fire and stored for use through the winter. Araucarias bear their first seeds when they are twenty-five years old and prolific groves were especially prized.

Kapok tree, Tambopata, Manu Biosphere Reserve, Peru

The kapok tree or ceiba (*Ceiba pentandra*), also known as the silk cotton tree, is in the family Bombacaceae together with the baobab. Ceiba is one of the most striking of the tropical rainforest trees, with its flanged buttress roots and smooth grey trunk, which ascends 50 metres through the forest before spreading to form a wide flattened crown above the main canopy. Such a tree is known as an emergent. High above the forest, the ceiba is bathed in full sunlight. It requires full sun to grow, and so is common in high light environments such as forest edges, river banks and disturbed areas created by extensive tree-falls. When a giant ceiba comes crashing down in a storm, it breaks a hole in the forest that is suddenly flooded with light. In this way, the germination and growth of more of its kind is stimulated. The trees grow fast — 3 metres (9 feet) a year. Before flowering, every five to ten years, the ceiba drops its leaves (as it does each dry season) giving its pollinators (bats) easy access to the flowers. The resulting fruits open on the tree and let fly thousands of fine seeds attached to silken threads which are picked up by the tropical winds to drift above the forest. Kapok, as the threads are known, is a useful fibre. The ceiba is sacred to the Mayan Indians, who believe that souls ascend to heaven by rising up a mythical ceiba whose branches are heaven itself.

Rainstorm, Tambopata Wildlife Reserve, Peru

Rain is a defining attribute of tropical rainforests. In the Amazon, the average rainfall exceeds 200 centimetres (80 inches) but some places receive nearly 10 metres (32 feet) of rain each year. The rainstorms that deliver this can be terrifying in their intensity, preceded as they are by strong winds and piling cumulus clouds, and accompanied by thunder and lightning. Fifty percent of the moisture that falls is returned to the atmosphere through evaporation and transpiration, creating a circling river of water in the sky that never reaches the true rivers of the land. It is the trees that are driving this system, and if they are removed, climatologists predict a breakdown in the patterns of rain and energy across the Amazon Basin, accompanied by massive soil erosion as the land is forced to take the full force of tropical storms.

TOP:

Tree trunk, Amazon Basin, Peru

The thorny protuberances on the trunk of this
prickly ash (*Zanthoxylum cinereum*) probably
evolved to prevent animals climbing the tree
to feed on its leaves or seeds, or to protect the
bark from grazing. Plants in tropical forests fight
a constant battle against predation by insects
and other animals. The most sophisticated
weapons are chemical. Tropical leaves may be
laced with drugs or poisons. These may be in
the form of alkaloids like cocaine or caffeine
which taste bitter or caustic; of insecticides,
and other poisons like cyanide; of chemicals
that mimic hormones and interfere with
predator breeding; or of latex, resins and gums
which glue up the mouth parts of insects before
they have time to start chewing. Some plants
have up to ninety different defence compounds
and strategies, combining chemical warfare with
mechanical defences such as spines and thorns.
There is seesaw evolution between plant and
animal as each progressively evolves to outwit
the latest tactic of the other. On balance, the
plants seem to be winning. Most leaves survive
uneaten — in one tropical forest studied only
seven per cent of animals (including insects)
depend on living plant material for food.

BOTTOM:

Tree trunk, Amazon Basin, Peru

This thorny-trunked tree (*Jacaratia digitata*) is a
member of the papaya family.

RIGHT: **Leaf with drip tips, Amazon Basin, Peru**

The leaves of many tropical rainforest plants, like this species of Cecropia, end in long points known as 'drip tips'. Leaves with this feature dry more quickly than those without because water is shed from them as liquid drops rather than having to be slowly evaporated. In an environment which receives as much rain as does a tropical forest, keeping leaves free of water is important, as it discourages the growth on leaves of tiny epiphytes known as microphylls. It also allows the leaf to begin transpiration again quickly after a rainstorm.

ABOVE: *Rauvolfia praecox* (central tree), Peru

More than twenty-five percent of modern lifesaving western medicines are derived from rainforest plants, but the survival of many species is threatened today by clearfelling for pastoral activities, and by global warming.

6

THE TREES OF OCEANIA

The volcanic islands of Hawaii constitute the northeastern point of Polynesia in the Pacific Ocean. There in cultivation can be seen tropical trees introduced from all the continents. Hawaii also has numerous endemic trees of its own. Koa (*Acacia koa*) is found on all the islands, especially from 600–2000 metres (2000–6500 feet), often growing with ohi'a (*Metrosideros polymorpha*), mamane (*Sophora chrysophylla*), and a'e (*Sapindus saponaria*). Olopua (*Nestegis sandwicensis*), is an endemic species of the family Oleaceae and is one of the most common Hawaiian native trees found growing in the lower forest zones. The State Tree of Hawaii is the candlenut or kukui (*Aleurites moluccana*), widely found throughout Oceania. The seeds contain oil suitable for soap, paint, and candles.

New Zealand lies entirely in temperate latitudes. Its tree flora contains a mixture of ancient Gondwana descendants as well as some later colonisers from the tropics. There are almost no indigenous trees in common with its neighbour, Australia. New Zealand has twenty species of conifer, including the kauri (*Agathis australis*) – a huge tree confined to the northern part of the North Island — and the more widely distributed podocarps such as rimu (*Dacrydium cupressinum*), totara (*Podocarpus totara*), and kahikatea (*Dacrycarpus dacrydioides*).

   The most abundant broadleaved trees in New Zealand are the southern beeches — red beech (*Nothofagus fusca*), silver beech (*N. menziesii*) and mountain beech (*N. solandri* var. *cliffortioides*) — which clothe the mountain slopes up to 1400 metres (4500 feet) elevation in almost pure stands. Numerous other kinds of broadleaved trees such as taraire (*Beilschmiedia tarairi*), tawa (*B. tawa*), puriri (*Vitex lucens*), kohekohe (*Dysoxylum spectabile*), rata (*Metrosideros robusta*, *M. umbellata*), kamahi (*Weinmannia racemosa*) and rewarewa (*Knightia excelsa*) are constituents of the lowland evergreen forest and are usually accompanied by conifers.

The glory of the northern coasts — pohutukawa (*Metrosideros excelsa*) — is known as the New Zealand Christmas tree, its blossoms giving a blaze of red colour in December. Its relative the kanuka (*Kunzea ericoides*) is an abundant coloniser of bare sites. The widespread kowhai (*Sophora chathamica* and *S. microphylla*) is one of New Zealand's few deciduous trees, and the designated National Flower. Only one palm reaches New Zealand — the nikau (*Rhopalostylis sapida*), but there are several, common, impressively large tree ferns, with mamaku (*Cyathea medullaris*) attaining 20 metres (66 feet) in height.

Pohutukawa (*Metrosideros excelsa*),
New Zealand

ABOVE: **Acacias, Australian outback**

There are over 1000 species of acacias in Australia. Most are small, multi-stemmed trees, and many of them are found in the harsh conditions of the interior.

LEFT: **Eucalyptus trunks, Australia**

The eucalypts are the best known of all Australian trees. There are around 88 species, which are widely distributed and range in size from small shrubs to forest giants.

Australia is a huge island (or isolated continent) of great geological antiquity. Much of the land is dry and impoverished, but supports a wonderful array of distinctive trees, the best known being the eucalypts of the genera *Eucalyptus*, *Angophora* and *Corymbia*. There are approximately 800 species, ranging from shrubs or multi-stemmed bushes called mallees, to tall forest and woodland trees. The tallest of all the world's flowering plants is mountain ash (*Eucalyptus regnans*), which on moist, fertile sites in Victoria and Tasmania can attain a height of 100 metres (328 feet). Lining the seasonally dry rivers of inland Australia is the picturesque river red gum (*E. camaldulensis*). In its various provenances or geographic races it and its cousin the forest red gum (*E. tereticornis*) has taken its place in fibre and firewood forestry plantations in many countries. Eucalypts can even be found in arid central Australia, the best known being the ghost gum (*Corymbia aparrerinja*) – a popular subject for artists and photographers. Eucalypts belong to the myrtle family (Myrtaceae), a group very well represented in Australia; just a handful of eucalypts occur elsewhere, notably in Papua New Guinea, the Philippines, and Indonesia.

Low-lying country along the north Queensland coast is the habitat for the attractive large paperbark trees of the genus *Melaleuca*, and the rainforests of the eastern seaboard have numerous kinds of satinash (*Syzygium*).

Acacias are even more numerous in Australia than eucalypts, totalling around 1000 species. Most, however, are multi-stemmed small trees of the interior, exemplified by mulga (*Acacia aneura*). Perhaps the biggest of them is blackwood (*A. melanoxylon*) which yields a fine cabinet timber.

The she-oaks (*Casuarina*) are another very distinctly Australian group of trees. They are conifer-like in appearance and grow on harsh sites of low fertility, low rainfall, or subject to periodic flooding. River she-oak (*Casuarina cunninghamiana*) can become a huge tree, as can be seen along the Murumbidgee River near Canberra, but the real surprise package is the desert she-oak (*Allocasuarina decaisneana*) which rises to an impressive height out of the desert sands around Ayers Rock (Uluru).

Another highly characteristic group of Australian trees belongs to the protea family (Proteaceae). They are mostly shrubs or small trees, but some are large trees such as coast banksia (*Banksia integrifolia*), silky oak (*Grevillea robusta*), northern silky oak (*Cardwellia sublimis*), and the attractively flowered firewheel tree (*Stenocarpus sinuatus*).

The conifers of Australia are of considerable interest. Of the ancient family Araucariaceae, Australia has two magnificent representatives of *Araucaria* – the hoop pine (*Araucaria cunninghamii*) and bunya bunya (*A. bidwillii*). It also has three species of kauri (*Agathis*), the famous Wollemi pine (*Wollemia nobilis*), and a distinctive type of cypress (*Callitris*).

Isolated Norfolk Island, a territory of Australia, has a tree of international fame – the Norfolk Island pine (*Araucaria heterophylla*). This conifer grows straight and tall, with wonderfully symmetrical branching, and is very popular as an avenue and street tree in temperate maritime climates. The island also has an impressive tree hibiscus – *Lagunaria patersonia*.

New Caledonia is one of the botanical gems of Oceania. An ancient chip off Gondwana, the territory has an impressive tree flora, including more than forty endemic conifers. The araucarias are well represented, with pin colonnaire (*Araucaria columnaris*) being the National Tree. It grows near the coast on limestone terrain – seen at its best on the Isle of Pines and in the Loyalty Islands. Other araucarias grow on serpentine soils, examples being *A. muelleri, A. rulei* and *A. bernieri*. There are also five species of *Agathis*, an example being the scrub kauri (*Agathis ovata)* which grows squat with a spreading crown above the scrubby serpentine.

Finally, there are a number of trees found on the coasts throughout tropical Oceania that are shared by all the islands and countries. Coconut (*Cocos nucifera*) is ubiquitous. Fish poison tree (*Barringtonia asiatica*) is a very well-known and widespread, exclusively coastal tree with a large spreading crown. The fruits float at sea. The beach almond (*Terminalia catappa*) has whorled branches, and the leaves turn red before falling. The ivi tree or Tahitian chestnut (*Inocarpus fagiferus)* has large plank buttresses and is found along stream banks throughout the tropical South Pacific and it can be one of the most common trees in riverine forests. *Calophyllum inophyllum* can be found on every Pacific shore – a handsome tree in every respect.

Podocarp forest, West Coast, New Zealand

Maori describe the productivity and health of the forest as being dependent on its 'mauri' or life principle. They would carefully conceal among the trees a specially selected natural object, such as an unusually shaped stone. By empowering the stone with prayers and chants, it became the dwelling place of forest spirits. A lizard would be released nearby to become the caretaker of the mauri. So long as the life principle of the forest was not violated, the forest would continue to be fruitful.

Oparara River, West Coast, New Zealand

The limestone rock base of the Oparara River has encouraged the formation of an exceptionally rich and diverse forest with high numbers of native birds. Underground rivers have carved a maze of caves beneath the forest and recently caches of extinct bird bones have been discovered — forest moas, giant eagles and numerous smaller birds that vanished when people and their attendant rats, dogs, cats and other predators reached mammal-free early New Zealand. The Oparara was the focus of a major conservation campaign (ultimately successful) in the 1980s to have it protected from logging.

Kanuka, Cape Farewell, New Zealand

Sheltered from sunlight and wind beneath the hardy pioneering kanuka (*Kunzea ericoides*), a forest can regenerate. The regenerative medicinal powers of kanuka were used extensively by Maori and early European settlers. Many parts of the tree were useful. Its leaves were infused for vapour baths, drunk to allay urinary complaints and fever, or decocted for stiff backs. The gum was applied to scalds and burns, or sucked to stop coughing. The bark was infused and drunk as a sedative or applied externally for skin diseases. The sap was taken as a blood purifier; the seed capsules boiled for diarrhoea or for colic and the young shoots eaten for dysentery.

ABOVE: **Southern beeches, winter frost, Marlborough, New Zealand**

LEFT: **Pohutukawa, East Cape, New Zealand**

The pohutukawa (*Metrosideros excelsa*) is a coastal tree in the North Island of New Zealand. The species is well adapted to salty sea mists and sandy soils. In December, the sombre grey-green trees burst into spectacular red flowers. Flowering pohutukawa are symbolic of Christmas and coastal summer holidays to New Zealanders. When the ancestral Maori voyaging canoe, Te Arawa, first came within sight of the New Zealand coast, the chief threw his sacred red headdress into the sea, declaring that the land's garland was more beautiful than his own.

Ivi tree, Tahiti

The snaking rivulet-shaped buttresses of the ivi tree (*Inocarpus fagiferus*)
are found along stream banks throughout the tropical South Pacific and it
can be one of the most common trees in riverine forests. The ivi is valued by
Pacific people wherever it grows. Its buttressed roots are used as drums and
the resulting deep thudding carries far in the forest. The large, green, single-
seeded pods are edible and are baked in stone ovens with grated coconut as a
forest delicacy. Weight for weight the ivi seed has over twice the energy value
of the sweet potato.

ABOVE: **Cootamundra wattle, New South Wales, Australia**

Early colonists to Australia, looking for house-building materials in the forests of their new land, found that the young saplings of acacias, including the popular ornamental Cootamundra wattle (*Acacia baileyana*), were ideal for use in weaving the wattle and mud daub walls of the house types they had made in England. The acacia stems were strong, pliant and resistant to decay. In time, the name 'wattle' was transferred to the acacias themselves.

RIGHT: **Brittle gum, Canberra Botanic Gardens, Australia**

Eucalyptus trees are characteristic of the Australian dry forests. They probably evolved from among the plants that specialised in colonising the margins of the ancient rainforest where soil nutrition was low and water was scarce. Over millennia, Australia became increasingly dry with major climatic changes, giving those trees which specialised in such conditions an ever-widening niche to expand into. Today, there are over 800 kinds of eucalypts, one of which is the brittle gum (*Eucalyptus mannifera*). Most are well adapted to surviving drought (with thick bark and leaves that hang vertically away from the sun to conserve water) and to surviving fires which ravage the dry lands (with highly flammable leaves which burn readily to clear the forest undergrowth but with thick bark to protect the sap wood).

Snow gum, Snowy Mountains, Australia

Snow gums (*Eucalyptus pauciflora*) are the only trees to grow above the snowline in Australia. With increasing altitude they become smaller and their leaves shorter until conditions are finally too harsh for survival. The seed of the snow gum is bigger than that of other gums to ensure a sufficient food store for the new seedling to survive germination and the first difficult weeks of life. It is the chance to feed on snowgum fruit that attracts gang gang cockatoos and the occasional flock of rosellas high into the snowy mountains of Australia.

Coconut palms, Tahiti

Ubiquitous on Pacific shores, the coconut tree is not only picturesque and shady, but yields a range of useful products – coconut oil, coconut cream, fibre for matting, and a useful timber from the trunk.

Mangrove trees, Queensland

Mangroves are not universally popular, but their huge ecological and economic significance is now becoming more widely recognised. The Queensland mangrove forests produce large quantities of leaves and other sources of nutrition, making them an extremely important coastal habitat for birds and many kinds of sealife.

Nikau palm, New Zealand

The nikau (*Rhopalostylis sapida*) is New Zealand's only palm tree, growing up to 15 metres (50 feet). The fruit takes a year to ripen into bright red clusters of berries that attract native birds in numbers.

Frangipani, Tahiti

The heavy scent of frangipani (*Plumeria* spp.) is most powerful at night in the tropics when glades of the tree can perfume the air for a great distance. Originally from the tropical forests of Central America, frangipani has been taken to countries around the world. In the Pacific, it is frequently planted in villages and is used in garlands and to scent coconut oil.

BELOW: **Coconut palms, Fiji**

COUNTRY	COMMON NAME	LATIN NAME
Australia	golden wattle	*Acacia pycnantha*
Alaska (USA)	Sitka spruce	*Picea sitchensis*
Argentina	ceibo	*Erythrina crista-galli*
Arizona (USA)	palo verde	*Cercidium floridum*
Arkansas (USA)	short-leaf pine	*Pinus echinata*
Belize	mahogany	*Swietenia macrophylla*
Bhutan	cypress	*Cupressus cashmeriana*
Bolivia	cantuta	*Cantua buxifolia*
Brazil	pau brasil	*Caesalpinia echinata*
Canada	sugar maple	*Acer saccharum*
China	ginkgo	*Ginkgo biloba*
Colombia	Andean wax palm	*Ceroxylon quindiuense*
Costa Rica	guanacaste	*Enterolobium cyclocarpum*
Cuba	royal palm	*Roystonea regia*
Delaware (USA)	American holly	*Ilex opaca*
Dominica	carib wood	*Poitea carinalis*
England	beech	*Fagus sylvatica*
France	yew	*Taxus baccata*
Georgia (USA)	live oak	*Quercus virginiana*
Germany	oak	*Quercus robur*
Hawaii (USA)	candlenut or kukui	*Aleurites moluccana*
Honduras	pino ocote	*Pinus oocarpa*
Idaho (USA)	western white pine	*Pinus monticola*
India	banyan	*Ficus benghalensis*
Israel	willow	*Salix*
Italy	field elm	*Ulmus minor*
Jamaica	lignum vitae	*Guaiacum officinale*
Lebanon	cedar	*Cedrus libani*
Madagascar	poinciana, flamboyant	*Delonix regia*

COUNTRY	COMMON NAME	LATIN NAME
Maine (USA)	eastern white pine	*Pinus strobus*
Malawi	Mulanje cedar	*Widdringtonia whytei*
Mexico	Mexican bald cypress or ahuehuete	*Taxodium mucronatum*
Minnesota (USA)	red pine	*Pinus resinosa*
Montana (USA)	ponderosa pine	*Pinus ponderosa*
Morocco	argan tree	*Argania spinosa*
Nepal	lali guras	*Rhododendron arboretum*
Nevada (USA)	single-leaf pinyon	*Pinus monophylla*
New Caledonia	pin colonnaire	*Araucaria columnaris*
New Zealand	kowhai	**Sophora microphylla*
Nicaragua	frangipani	*Plumeria alba*
North Carolina (USA)	longleaf pine	*Pinus palustris*
Ohio (USA)	buckeye	*Aesculus glabra*
Paraguay	lapacho	*Tabebuia heptaphylla*
Pennsylvania (USA)	eastern hemlock	*Tsuga canadensis*
Peru	quinine	*Cinchona calisaya*
Peru	cantuta	**Cantua buxifolia*
Philippines	narra	*Pterocarpus indicus*
Puerto Rico	maga	*Montezuma speciosissima*
Russia	birch	*Betula pubescens, B. pendula*
South Africa	real yellowwood	*Podocarpus latifolius*
Sri Lanka	na	*Mesua ferrea*
Tennessee (USA)	tulip tree	*Liriodendron tulipifera*
Texas (USA)	pecan	*Carya illinoinensis*
Uruguay	ceibo	*Erythrina crista-galli*
USA	oak	*Quercus alba*
Utah (USA)	blue spruce	*Picea pungens*
Washington (USA)	western hemlock	*Tsuga heterophylla*
Wisconsin (USA)	sugar maple	*Acer saccharum*

INDEX

a'e 141
Abies 11, 53
Abies alba 17
Abies amabilis 99
Abies balsamea 101
Abies cephalonica 18
Abies cilicica 18
Abies grandis 99
Abies lasiocarpa 101
Abies nordmanniana 18
Abies pinsapo 18
acacia 11, 75, 91, 142, 143
Acacia 11, 12
Acacia albida 75
Acacia aneura 143
Acacia x anthophloea 75, 79, 82
Acacia baileyana 149
Acacia dealbata 14
Acacia erioloba 75, 84
Acacia giraffe 75
Acacia karroo 75
Acacia koa 141
Acacia melanoxylon 143
Acacia pycnantha 156
Acacia senegal 75
Acacia sieberana 75, 83
Acacia tortilis 75
Acer campestre 18
Acer grandidentata 99
Acer negundo 101
Acer palmatum 62
Acer platanoides 18, 50
Acer pseudoplatanus 18
Acer rubrum 101
Acer saccharum 101 , 156, 157
Acmena smithii 14
Adansonia digitata 76, 87
Aesculus glabra 157
afara 75
African mahogany 75
African tulip tree 76
Agathis 143
Agathis australis 9, 141
Agathis ovata 143
ahuehuete 126
Ailanthus altissima 14
akamatsu 59
Alaska 156
alder 18, 39, 121
Aleppo pine 17
alerce 126
Aleurites moluccana 14, 141, 156
Allocasuarina decaisneana 143
Alluaudia ascendens 76
Alluaudia procera 76
Alnus glutinosa 18
Alnus rubra 99
aloe 75
Aloe barberae 75
Aloe dichotoma 96
Alphen 11
Alps 36
Amazon 126, 137, 138, 139
American chestnut 15
American elm 15
American holly 156
Andean wax palm 156
Andes 126
angiosperms 10
Angophora 143
angsana 55
Anhui Province 53, 55
Appalachian Mountains 101
araguana 125
araucaria 125, 130, 143
Araucaria angustifolia 126
Araucaria araucana 126, 130, 132
Araucaria bernieri 143
Araucaria bidwillii 143
Araucaria columnaris 143, 157
Araucaria cunninghamii 143
Araucaria heterophylla 143
Araucaria muelleri 143
Araucaria rulei 143
Araucaria trees 135
Arbutus menziesii 99
Arbutus unedo 18
argan tree 76, 157

Argania spinosa 76, 157
Argentina 125, 127, 156
Arizona 112, 113, 156
Arkansas 156
Arolla pine 17, 32
Artocarpus heterophyllus 53
ash 18, 40
aspen 18, 99, 101
Atchafalaya Basin, Louisiana 110
Atlas cedar 76
Atlas Mountains 76
Aucoumea klaineana 75
Australia 142, 143, 149, 150, 156
Australian broadleaf paperbark 14
Austria 22, 31, 32, 42
Austrocedrus chilensis 126
Azadirachta indica 53
Bahamas 126
Baikiaea plurijuga 75
bald cypress 110
Balkans 17
balsa 135
balsam fir 101
bamboo 55, 73, 86
Bambusa oldhamii 55
Bambusa vulgaris 55
Banksia integrifolia 143
banyan 55, 156
banyan fig 65
baobab 76, 87, 89
Barringtonia asiatica 143
Bauhinia x blakeana 55
Bavaria 26, 32
bay laurel 18
beach almond 143
beech 18, 32, 35, 38, 42, 47, 50, 101, 125, 129, 156
Beilschmiedia tarairi 141
Beilschmiedia tawa 141
Belarus 17
Belize 156
Bertholletia excelsa 126
Betula 11
Betula papyrifera 101, 107
Betula pendula 18, 157
Betula pubescens 18, 157
Bhutan 156
Bialowieza National Park 17
big-leaved maple 99
birch 11, 18, 34, 40, 101, 157
black cottonwood 99
Black Forest 4, 17, 35, 38
black locust 101
black pine 17
black poplar 18
Black Sea 18
black spruce 101
black tupelo 101
black walnut 101
blackwood 143
Blakeana variegata 55
blue spruce 157
bo tree 55
Bolivia 125, 126, 156
Bombacopsis quinata 125
Borneo 55
Bosnian pine 17
boxelder maple 101
Brachystegia 11
Brazil 125, 126, 156
Brazil nut 126
Brazilian rosewood 125
bristlecone pine 114
Britain 17
brittle gum 149
broadleaved mahogany 126
buckeye 157
Bulawayo 86
bunya bunya 143
bur oak 101
Burmese banyan 71
butternut 101
cabbage trees 10
Caesalpinia echinata 125, 156
Caesalpinia ferrea 125
California 108, 109, 117, 121
California laurel 99
Californian redwood 108

Callitris 143
Calophyllum inophyllum 143
camel thorn 75, 84, 86, 95
Camellia 60
Cameroon Highlands 60
Cameroon 75
Canada 107, 156
Canary Islands 17
Canberra 143
Canberra Botanic Gardens 149
candelabra tree 75, 76
candlenut 14, 141, 156
Cantua buxifolia 156, 157
cantuta 156, 157
Cape Farewell 146
Cape Leeuwin 14
Cape Town 93
Cardwellia sublimis 143
carib wood 125, 156
Caribbean pine 126
carob 18
Carpathian Mountains 17
Carpinus betulus 18
Carya illinoensis 157, 101
Carya ovata 101
Cascade Ranges 99
Cassia javanica 55
Castanea dentata 15
Castanea sativa 18
castanho-do-Pará 126
Casuarina 143
Casuarina cunninghamiana 14,143
Casuarina equisetifolia 14
Casuarina glauca 14
Caucasian fir 18
cedar 156
cedar of Lebanon 18
Cedrus atlantica 76
Cedrus libani 18, 156
ceiba 126, 137
Ceiba pentandra 125, 137
ceibo 125, 156, 157
Central Africa 11
Central America 125, 126
Central Park, New York 122
Ceratonia siliqua 18
Cercidium floridum 156
Ceroxylon quindiuense 126, 156
Chamaecyparis obtusa 53
cherry laurel 18
chestnut 18
Chile 125, 128, 129, 130, 132, 135
Chilean cedar 126
Chilean monkey-puzzles 130
China 15, 55, 56, 64, 156
Chinese camphor 14
Chinese fir 53
Chinese red pine 53
Chorisia speciosa 125
Cinchona calisaya 126, 157
Cinnamomum camphora 14
coast banksia 143
coast redwood 9, 99, 108
coconut palm 12, 70, 143, 151, 155
Cocos nucifera 12, 143
coigüe 126
Colombia 126, 156
Colophospermum mopane 75
common elm 15
common lime 18
common wild fig 81
Conguillio National Park 128
conifers 9, 39 143
Cook Islands 76
Cootamundra wattle 149
Cordyline 10
cork oak 18
Corsican pine 17
Corylus avellana 18
Corymbia 143
Corymbia aparrerinja 143
Costa Rica 156
crack willow 14, 18
Cryptomeria japonica 53, 65
Cuba 126, 156
Cuban mahogany 126
Cunninghamia lanceolata 53
Cupressus cashmeriana 156

Cupressus macrocarpa 121
Cupressus sempervirens 18, 24
Cyathea medullaris 141
cycads 8
cypress 25, 143, 156
Dacrycarpus dacrydioides 1412
Dacrydium cupressinum 141
Dalbergia nigra 125
dawn redwood 53
deciduous trees 18
Delaware 156
Delonix regia 12, 76, 156
desert she-oak 143
dicotyledons 10
Didierea madagascariensis 76
dika 75
Dipterocarpus 55
dogwood 46
Dolomite Mountains 17, 44
Dominica 156
Douglas fir 9, 99
downy birch 18
Dracaena hookeriana 93
dracaenas 10
dragon tree 93
Drakensberg Mountains 13, 75
Dryobalanops 55
duiker nut 75
durango pine 126
Dutch elm 18
Dypsis decaryi 76
Dysoxylum spectabile 141
East Cape 147
eastern hemlock 101, 157
eastern white pine 101, 157
elm 18
Eng Valley 22, 31
Engelmann spruce 114; Englemann spruce 101[check correct spelling]
England 15, 28, 34, 40, 156
English oak 28
Entandrophragma cylindricum 75
Entandrophragma utile 75
Enterolobium cyclocarpum 156
Erythrina crista-galli 125, 156, 157
eucalypts 142, 143, 149
Eucalyptus 11, 12, 143
Eucalyptus camaldulensis 11, 143
Eucalyptus mannifera 149
Eucalyptus pauciflora 150
Eucalyptus regnans 143
Eucalyptus tereticornis 143
Euphorbia ingens 75, 76
European Alps 17
European beech 18
European larch 17, 36
European white fir 17
evergreen buckthorn 18
Fagus crenata 66
Fagus grandifolia 101
Fagus orientalis 18
Fagus sylvatica 18, 156
Faidherbia 75
Faidherbia albida 75
ferns 8
fever tree 75, 79, 82
Ficus 55
Ficus benghalensis 55, 156
Ficus ingens 87
Ficus natalensis 81
Ficus religiosa 55
Ficus sycamorus 88
field elm 156
field maple 18
fig tree 55, 81
Fiji 155
fir 39
firewheel tree 143
fish poison tree 143
Fizroya cupressoides 126
flamboyant poinciana 76
Florida 156
floss-silk tree 125
Fontainebleau Forest 23
forest red gum 143
France 17, 23, 49, 156
frangipani 155, 157
Fraxinus angustifolia 18

Fraxinus excelsior 18, 40
Fraxinus latifolia 99
Fraxinus pennsylvanica 101
French Guiana 126
Gabon 75
Gaboon mahogany 75
Georgia 156
Germany 17, 26, 29, 32, 35, 38, 156
ghost gum 143
giant redwood 9
giant sequoia 99, 109

Ginkakuji Temple 67
ginkgo 9, 53, 69, 156
Ginkgo biloba 8, 9, 53, 156
Glen Affric 34
golden wattle 156
Grand Canyon 112, 113
grand fir 99
Great Basin National Park 114
Grecian fir 18
Greek juniper 18
green ash 101
Grevillea robusta 143
grey willow 14
Guaiacum officinale 156
guanacaste 156
guava 14
gum Arabic tree 75
gymnosperms 8, 9
hairy bamboo 55
halfmens plant 75, 92
Hampshire 28
Hangzchou 15
Hawaii 141, 156
hawthorn 46
hazel 18, 46
headache tree 99
hedgerow 46
Hester Malan Nature Reserve 92
Hevea brasiliensis 12, 126
hinoki 53
Hinterriss 42
Hirosaki 9, 66, 69
holly 18
holm oak 18
Honduran mahogany 126
Honduras 156
Hong Kong 55
Hong Kong orchid tree 55
Honshu 4, 56, 66, 68
hoop pine 143
hornbeam 18
Huangshan 55, 64
Idaho 156
Iguassú Falls 126, 127
Ilex aquifolium 18
Ilex opaca 156
India 53, 55, 156
Indonesia 143
Inocarpus fagiferus 143, 148
ironwood 53
Irvingia gabonensis 75
Isle of Pines 143
Israel 156
Italy 17, 24, 25, 27, 44, 156
ivi tree 143, 148
jacaranda 12, 125
Jacaranda mimosifolia 12, 125
Jacaratia digitata 138
jack pine 101
jakfruit 53
Jamaica 156
Japan 4, 9, 53, 56, 58, 59, 62, 63, 65, 66, 67, 68, 69, 73
Japanese beech 66
Japanese black pine 59, 63, 67
Japanese cedar 65
Japanese maple 62
Japanese red pine 59
Jefferson Island 111
Joshua tree 117
Juglans cinerea 101
Juglans nigra 101
Juglans regia 12
Julbernandia 11
Juniperus communis 18
Juniperus drupacea 18

Juniperus excelsa 18
Juniperus foetidissima 18
Juniperus oxycedrus 18
kahikatea 141
Kalahari 75
kamahi 141
kanuka 141, 146
kapok 125
kapok tree 137
Karwendel Mountains 22, 31, 32
kauri 9, 141, 143
Kenya 76, 78, 79, 91, 93, 95
kermes oak 18
Khaya ivorensis 75
Kiev 29
Kigelia pinnata 76, 78
Kirstenbosch Botanical Gardens 93
Knightia excelsa 141
koa 141
kohekohe 141
Kokerboom Forest 4, 96
kowhai 141, 157
Kruger National Park 75
kukui 141
Kunzea ericoides 141, 146
kuromatsu 59
Kyoto 59, 67
Lagerstroemia speciosa 55
Lagunaria patersonia 143
Lake Christabel 4
Lake Conguillio 125
Lake District, Chile 127, 129
Lake Mjøsa 39
lali guras 157
lapacho 125, 157
larch 32, 39, 50, 53
Larix 11, 53
Larix europaea 17
Larix laricina 101
Laurus nobilis 18
Lebanon 156
lenga 126
leopard tree 125
Lepidozamia hopei 8
Leucadendron argenteum 93
Leucaena leucocephala 14
lignum vitae 156
Ligustrum lucidum 14
lillypilly 14
Limpopo River 75
linden 18
liquidambar 53
Liquidambar styraciflua 101
Liriodendron tulipifera 101, 157
Lithocarpus densiflorus 99
live oak 101, 111, 156
Llaima Volcano 130
loblolly pine 101
Loch Awe 43
lodgepole pine 14, 101
Loire Valley 49
longleaf pine 101, 157
Lonquimay Volcano 135
Louisiana 111
Loyalty Islands 143
Macedonian pine 17
Madagascar 76, 156
maga 125, 157
Magnolia grandiflora 101
mahogany 126, 156
Maine 104, 157
Malawi 76, 157
Malaysia 55, 60, 70
mamaku 141
mamane 141
Mangifera indica 53
mango 53
mangroves 11, 152
Manu Biosphere Reserve 137
mao zhu 55
maple 46, 62, 104
maquis 18
maritime pine 14, 17
markhamia 76
Markhamia lutea 76
Marlborough, New Zealand 147
marula trees 85
Maso-chiku bamboo forest 73

Masson pine 53
Mediterranean 17
Mediterranean cypress 18, 24
Melaleuca 143
Melaleuca quinquenervia 14
Messina 87
Mesua ferrea 53, 157
Metasequoia glyptostroboides 53
Metrosideros excelsa 141, 147 ;
Metrosideros polymorpha 141
Metrosideros robusta 141
Metrosideros umbellata 141
Mexican bald cypress 9, 126, 157
Mexico 9, 126, 157
Minnesota 157
Miombo region 11
Mojave Desert 117
monkey breadfruit 76
monkey pod 125
monkey puzzle tree 126, 132
monocotyledons 10
Montana 157
Monterey cypress 121
Montezuma speciosissima 125, 157
Moroccan ironwood 76
Morocco 76, 157
moso bamboo 55
mountain ash 39, 143
mountain beech 141
mountain pine 32
Muir Woods 99
Mulanje cedar 76, 157
mulga 143
Murumbidgee River 143
Myanmar 53, 55
na 53
Namib Desert 84, 86
Namibia 4, 84, 85, 86, 96
narra 55, 157
narrow-leaved mahogany 126
Natal 83
Natal mahogany 81
Ndumo 81, 82
neem 53
Nepal 157
Nestegis sandwicensis 141
Netherlands 11
Neuschwanstein Castle 26
Nevada 99, 114, 157
New Caledonia 143, 157
New England 101, 104
New Guinea 55
New South Wales 149
New York State 101
New Zealand 4, 9, 10, 141, 146, 147, 153, 157
New Zealand Christmas tree 141
Nicaragua 157
nikau palm 141, 153
Norfolk Island 143
Norfolk Island pine 143
North Carolina 157
North Yorkshire Dales 40
Northern Honshu 53
northern red oak 101
northern silky oak 143
Northern Transvaal 85
Norway 39, 50
Norway maple 18, 50
Norway spruce 17, 32
Nothofagus 11, 127
Nothofagus dombeyi 126
Nothofagus fusca 141
Nothofagus menziesii 141
Nothofagus oblique 126
Nothofagus procera 126
Nothofagus pumilio 126
Nothofagus solandri var. *cliffortioides* 141
Nyssa aquatica 101
oak 76, 101, 156, 157
Oaxaco 9
obeche 75
Ochroma pyramidale 125
ohi'a 141
Ohio 157
Oirase Valley 4, 53, 58, 68
Oirasegawa River 66
okoume 75

old man's beard lichen 132
Olea europaea 18
olive tree 18, 44
Olopua 141
Olympic Peninsula 99
Oparara River 146
Oregon ash 99
oriental spruce 18
Pachira quinata 125
Pachypodium namaquanum 75, 92
Pacific madrone 99
Pacific silver fir 99
padauk 55
palms 10, 126, 141
palo verde 156
paper birch 101, 107
paperbark acacia 75, 83
paperbark trees 143
Papua New Guinea 143
Paraguay 125, 157
parana pine 126
pau brasil 125, 156
pecan 101, 157
pedunculate oak 18
Pennsylvania 157
Peru 125, 126, 137, 138, 139, 157
Philippines 55, 143, 157
Phyllostachys edulis 55, 73
Phyllostachys vivax 'Aureocaulis' 86
Picea 11, 53
Picea abies 17
Picea engelmannii 101, 114
Picea glauca 101
Picea mariana 101
Picea omorika 18
Picea orientalis 18
Picea pungens 157
Picea sitchensis 9, 99, 156
pin colonnaire 143, 157
pin oak 101
pindó 126
pine 32, 34, 39, 64, 132
pink shower tree 55
pino ocote 156
piñon pine 113
Pinus 11, 12
Pinus aristata 114
Pinus banksiana 101
Pinus brutia 17
Pinus canariensis 17
Pinus caribaea var. *bahamensis* 126
Pinus caribaea var. *caribaea* 126
Pinus caribaea var. *hondurensis* 126
Pinus cembra 17
Pinus contorta 14, 99, 101
Pinus densata 53
Pinus densiflora 59
Pinus durangensis 126
Pinus echinata 156
Pinus edulis 113
Pinus eliottii 101
Pinus halepensis 17
Pinus heldreichii 17
Pinus lambertiana 99
Pinus massoniana 53
Pinus monophylla 157
Pinus monticola 99, 156
Pinus mugo 17
Pinus nigra 17
Pinus nigra subsp. *laricio* 17
Pinus oocarpa 156
Pinus palustris 101, 157
Pinus peuce 17
Pinus pinaster 14, 17
Pinus pinea 17
Pinus ponderosa 101, 157
Pinus radiata 12
Pinus resinosa 157
Pinus strobus 101, 157
Pinus sylvestris 17, 21
Pinus tabuliformis 53
Pinus taeda 101
Pinus taiwanensis 53
Pinus thunbergii 59, 63, 67
Pinus yunnanensis 53
plane trees 15
Platanus occidentalis 101
Platanus orientalis 11

Plumeria 155
Plumeria alba 157
pochote 125, 126
podocarps 144
Podocarpus latifolius 76, 157
Podocarpus totara 141
pohutukawa 141, 147
poinciana 12, 76, 156
Point Lobos 121
Poitea carinalis 125, 156
Poland 17
ponderosa pine 101, 112, 119, 157
poplar 11
Populus 11, 12
Populus euphratica 11
Populus nigra 18
Populus tremula 18
Populus tremuloides 101, 107
Populus trichocarpa 99
prickly ash 138
pride of Bolivia 125
Pride of India 55
protea 75, 143
Protea caffra 75
Prunus laurocerasus 18
Pseudotsuga menziesii 9, 99
Psidium guajava 14
Pterocarpus indicus 155, 157
Puerto Rico 125, 157
puriri 141
Pyrenees 17
quaking aspen 107
Quebec 102, 107
queen palm 126, 127
queen's crepe myrtle 55
Queensland 143, 152
Quercus alba 101, 157
Quercus canariensis 76
Quercus coccifera 18
Quercus coccinea 101
Quercus faginea 76
Quercus falcata 101
Quercus ilex 18
Quercus macrocarpa 101
Quercus palustris 101
Quercus petraea 17, 18
Quercus pyrenaica 76
Quercus robur 18, 156
Quercus rubra 15, 101
Quercus shumardii 101
Quercus suber 18
Quercus virginiana 101, 111, 156
quinine 126, 157
quiver trees 96
rain tree 12, 125
Rarotonga 76
rata 141
rauli 126
Rauvolfia praecox 139
real yellowwood 76, 157
red alder 99
red beech 141
red maple 101
red oak 101
red pine 157
rewarewa 141
Rhamnus alaternus 18
Rhodesian teak 75
Rhododendron arboretum 157
Rhopalostylis sapida 141, 153
rimu 141
river red gum 143
river she-oak 143
Robinia pseudoacacia 101
roble 126
rock fig 87
Rocky Mountains 101
Rokuon-ji Garden 59
rosewood 55
rowan 18, 39
rowan berries 39
royal palm 126, 156
Roystonea regia 126, 156
rubber tree 12, 126
Russia 17, 157
sabinea 125
Sahelian Africa 75
Salix 156

Salix cinerea 14
Salix fragilis 14, 18
Samanea saman 12, 125
sapele 75
Sapindus saponaria 141
satinash 143
sausage tree 76, 78
scarlet oak 101
Sclerocarya birrea 85
Scotland 21, 34, 43, 47
Scots pine 17, 21
scrub kauri 143
Senegalia 75
Sequoia sempervirens 9, 99, 108
Sequoiadendron giganteum 9, 99, 109
Serbian spruce 18
sessile oak 17, 18
shagbark hickory 101
Sheffield Park 15, 34
she-oak 14, 143
shore pine 99
Shorea 55
short-leaf pine 156
Shumard oak 101

Sierra Nevada Mountains 99
silk cotton tree 137
silk kapok tree 125
silky oak 143
silver beech 141
silver firs 38
silver tree 93
silver wattle 14
Singapore 65, 71
single-leaf pinyon 157
sipo 75
Sirerra redwood 99
sitka spruce 9, 99, 156
slash pine 101
Slovenia 17
Smuggler's Notch 107
snow gum 150
Snowdonia National Park 18
Snowy Mountains 150
Solomons 55
Sophora chathamica 141
Sophora chrysophylla 141
Sophora microphylla 141, 157
Sorbus aria 18
Sorbus aucuparia 18
South Africa 9, 13, 75, 76, 81, 82, 83, 85, 87, 88, 92, 93, 157
southern beech 126, 127, 141, 147
southern magnolia 101
southern red oak 101
Spanish fir 18
Spanish moss 101, 110
Spathodea campanulata 76
spindle 346
spiny octopus tree 76
spruce 35, 39, 50, 53

Sri Lanka 53, 157
Stenocarpus sinuatus 143
stone pine 17
strawberry tree 18
subalpine fir 101
sugar maple 101, 156, 157
sugar pine 99
sugi 53
swamp cypress 101, 110
Swaziland 87
Sweden 40
sweet gum 101
sweet thorn 75
Swietenia macrophylla 126, 156
Swietenia mahogoni 126
Swiss mountain pine 17
Swiss stone pine 17
Switzerland 36, 50
Syagrus romanzoffiana 126, 127
sycamore 101
sycamore fig 88
sycamore maple 18
Syrian juniper 18
Syzygium 143

Tabebuia chrysantha 125
Tabebuia chrysotricha 125
Tabebuia heptaphylla 125, 157
Tahiti 148, 151, 155
Tahitian chestnut 143
taiga 39
tamarack 101
tamarind 53
Tamarindus indica 53
Tambopata Wildlife Reserve 137
tan oak 99
taraire 141
Tasmania 143
Taurus fir 18
tawa 141
Taxodium distichum 101, 110
Taxodium mucronatum 9, 126, 157
Taxus baccata 156
tea plantation 60
teak 53
Tectona grandis 53
Tennessee 157
Terminalia catappa 143
Terminalia superba 75
Tetraclinis articulata 76
Texas 157
Thailand 53, 55
thorny-trunked tree 138
Thuja plicata 99
Tilia x europaea 18
Tilia heterophylla 101
Tillandsia usneoides 110
tipa tree 125
Tipuana tipu 125
topiary 49
totara 141

Towada Hachimantai National Park 56
Transvaal 76, 88
tree ferns 8, 9, 141
tree hibiscus 143
tree of heaven 14
tree privet 14
triangle palm 76
Trichilia emetica 81
Triplochiton scleroxylon 75
Tsuga canadensis 101, 157
Tsuga heterophylla 99, 157
Tulé 126
Tulé cypress 9
tulip tree 101, 157
Turkey 17, 18
Turkish pine 17
Tuscany 25, 44
Ukraine 29
Ulmus americana 15
Ulmus carpinifolia 18
Ulmus glabra 15, 18
Ulmus x hollandica 15, 18
Ulmus laevis 18
Ulmus minor 156
Ulmus procera 15
Umbellularia californica 99
umbrella thorn 75, 83, 130
Umbria 24, 27
Urewera National Park 10
Uruguay 125, 157
Usnea 132
Utah 119, 157
utile 75
Vachellia 75
Varmland 40
Venezuela 125, 126
Vermont 100, 101, 104, 107, 121
Vestfold 39, 50
Victoria 143
Victoria Falls 81
Vietnam 55
Villandry Chateau 49
Vitex lucens 141
Waipoua Forest 9
Wales 4, 18, 46
walnut tree 12
Washington 157
water tupelo 101
wax palm 126
weeping willow 56
Weinmannia racemosa 141
West Africa 75
West Coast, New Zealand 144, 146
West Indies 125, 126
West Lake, Hangzhou 56
western hemlock 99, 157
western red cedar 99
western white pine 99, 156
Wheeler Peak 114
white basswood 101
White Mountains 114
white oak 101
white pine 101
white spruce 101
whitebeam 128
Widdringtonia whytei 76, 157
willow 156
Wisconsin 157
Wollemi pine 143
Wollemia nobilis 143
wych elm 15
Yamadera 63, 65
Yellow Mountain pine 53
Yellow Mountains 53
yellow trumpet flower 125
yew 49, 156
Yosemite National Park 109
Yucca brevifolia 117
yucca 10
Yunnan 53
Zambezi River Gorge 80
Zambia 80
Zanthoxylum cinereum 138
zapote 126
Zimbabwe 81, 86, 89
Zion National Park, Utah 117, 119
Zuurberg cycad 9
Zuurberg National Park 9